Hell Desk To Help Desk

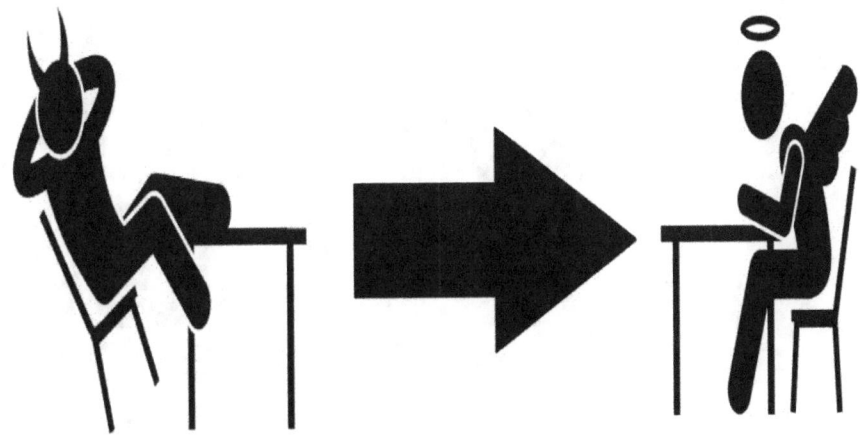

Salvation For Your IT Support

Brian P McCoppin

Dedication

This book is for my wife.

The wife who tolerates the nerd that I am.

This is a thank you for supporting me on those late nights and long weekends. For your patience when I got those 2AM phone calls. I could not have done this without your love and support.

This book was your idea. You are my muse, my life, and my Angel as I fought my way through these hells.

Contents

The Hell of IT 1
The Seven Circles of IT Hell 9
The Hell of This Book 11
The Hell of IT Expenditure 15
The Hell of Impressions 29
The Hell of an Uneducated Employee 43
The Hell of Expectations 55
The Hell of Hiring, Training, and Firing 65
The Hell of Culture 79
The Hell of Leadership 91
IT Heaven 101
Index 1 - The IT Demons 111
Index 2 - The Non-IT Demons 115
Index 3 - The IT Saints 119
Index 4 - References 123
Index 5 - Further Reading 127
About the Author 129

The Hell of IT

We have all been there. You go to open a file from the report you have spent the last three months working on, and you get the dreaded error: 'File Not Found.' Panic hits. Hundreds of hours of work spent on this project are now in peril. Countless dollars are at risk of being lost. Worst of all, your career is now in jeopardy. You immediately dive for your cell phone and dial the company's help desk. The phone rings seven times and then goes to voicemail.

"Please," you beg over the phone, "please call me back. I need this report."

Minutes tick by, but no one has returned your call. Realization hits… it's Sunday, and you need to call a different number on weekends. But w*here is that 'on call' number?* You scroll through your call history in a hurry. You try three wrong numbers before you get the correct one.

"Thank you for calling; please leave a message, and an agent will return your call."

You start to see red. What good is an 'on call' number if it goes to voicemail?

"Please call me back; I cannot open this report that's due tomorrow." You click the phone dead in frustration. After five minutes, you call again. Voice mail.

Hell Desk To Help Desk

I'll call the IT manager. They can get someone to help me. You start to look through your phone for the IT Department's manager. You have called them enough times, so you know the number is here somewhere. Finally, there it is. You call the manager's number. Voicemail again! You can feel the vein popping out on your forehead.

Who is the IT manager's boss?

Your computer beeps. There is a message from the IT support group. "Hey, I saw you called. Sup?"

Sup!? SUP!?!?! You take a deep breath and type a message back.

You: "I cannot find a report. Can you help me find it?"

IT: "Have you tried rebooting yet?"

You: "No, I just need a file, the computer seems ok."

IT: "Do me a solid and reboot. Send me a message once the computer is back on."

Fine, I will do whatever just to get this file.

You: "OK."

You reboot your computer, and it opens to a blue screen: 'Performing updates, estimated time 25 minutes.'

You call the on-call number again. Voicemail again.

The next two hours are pure agony. Your computer reboots six times while applying the updates, sometimes failing and starting over again. Visions of your family destitute and begging for money flash through your mind. The updates finish, and it finally lets you in. You log into your laptop.

"Your account password is expired. Please call your IT support for assistance."

You blackout.

This sounds like a horrible experience, right? Your career is at risk, and those paid to support you show no signs of giving a damn.

Let's fast forward an hour. You finally get IT on the phone.

IT: "Ok, your file opened. Need anything else?"
You: "No, we look good."

You hang up the phone. You are still angry. You want someone to yell at. This was three hours wasted on your Sunday.

I hate our IT support team.

The team solved your problem, as they eventually seem to usually do, but why was it so painful? Why did you have to call two numbers? Why did the on-call tech message back and not call back? Why did the updates take so long? Why did your password get locked out?

Let's flip this coin and see the other side.

You are an IT support tech at a medium-sized company. The Help Desk has only four agents supporting calls and incoming requests from 5,000 users. You are on call for the second week in a row since one of your four fellow agents is out on long-term medical leave, and HR won't let your team backfill as the company still has to pay their salary while out and there is no budget for a fifth agent.

You haven't left your computer screen in weeks. Your company employees need constant support, day or night, and your team has a backlog of three hundred tickets to follow up on. You have only averaged four hours of sleep a night throughout the last month.

Hell Desk To Help Desk

You and your family are driving to church this Sunday. Your spouse has to drive because you are on your laptop *and* the phone helping a salesperson with a password reset. There are five new missed calls and one new voicemail, bringing your total of unread voicemails to three, just from the drive alone. You finally arrive. You kiss your spouse and hug your kids as they go inside, and you stay in the car. You roll down the window to catch that nice August breeze. You finally get the salesperson's password unique enough to take in all systems, so you finish the call.

You listen to the voicemails. The first user is another expired password, the second is a computer locked in an update loop, and the third is a manager looking for a missing report.

You call back the first user, password expired. *This should be a quick fix.* You see the third user is online on the company chat program, so you message them. You remember your leader coaching you on being more casual and friendly while supporting end users. You type the most friendly and casual message you can.

You: "Hey, I saw you called. Sup?"

Manager: "I cannot find a report. Can you help me find it?"

You recall that there is an issue with the file share, and reboots can fix the connection.

You: "Have you tried rebooting yet?"

Manager: "No, I just need a file, the computer seems ok."

You: "Do me a solid and reboot. Send me a message once the computer is back on."

Manager: "OK."

You see their account go offline. The user with the password lockout did not answer, so you call the one with the update loop issue. You spend the next thirty minutes doing nothing more than listening to a user turn off their laptop, turn it back on, and watch the updates. The user will not let you go until the laptop is working. Two more voicemails roll in while assisting this user.

You miss church. You are on the phone while the family eats at the only place nearby with outdoor seating, so you can at least be near them while working and not bother anyone else while talking on the phone.

You finally get the last voicemail taken care of. You haven't heard back from that manager with the missing file. You decide to finish your meal before checking if they are back online. Before your bill is paid, your on-call cell rings.

"Hey," you think it's the manager, "I rebooted like you asked and it took two hours to update my machine and now my password is locked!"

You roll your eyes. Another user who hasn't rebooted in months.

They are angry; you can hear it clearly in their voice.

"Ok," you respond, trying your best to smile and sound friendly, "let's get it working. What is your username?"

After working with the user, you find out their cellphone has an old password and caused the lockout. You are able to reset their password, and they can then get logged in. They find the file, and it opens.

You: "Ok, your file opened. Need anything else?"

Manager: "No, we look good."

They hang up without even saying thanks.

I hate my job.

Do you relate to either person? Are you the employee who dreads dealing with IT? Or are you the IT support who is overworked and underappreciated?

Hell Desk To Help Desk

Why do so many companies and organizations have IT support that sucks? What mindset leads companies to this? This book is comprised of stories from real people in real situations. We have seen IT team transformation that can only be called miraculous. Everything in this book has happened and will happen again. We see the same mistakes over and over again.

In this book, we will break down the root cause of these issues and guide you from transforming your Hell Desk to a Help Desk.

What this book is not: we do not recommend anything specific to buy in these pages. Do not come here expecting recommendations on specific software or hardware. There are dozens of excellent and tenfold more horrible solutions suited to many of the IT needs out there. We do, however, go over the required software types for a successful help desk. You can read these recommendations in the chapter, "The Hell of IT Expenditure."

A skilled and dedicated IT leader will know the best solutions for their team. To learn more about this capable leader, check out the chapter, "The Hell of Leadership."

Now, on to the Hells!

The Seven Circles of IT Hell

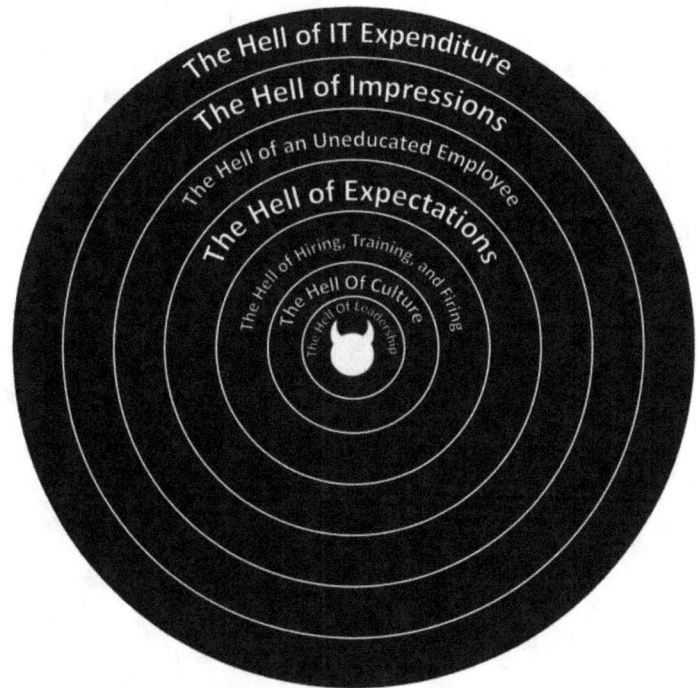

The Hell of This Book

In this book, we will introduce a fictional company and fictional employees. Every single employee we introduce is based on a real person or a conglomeration of people. You, the reader, whose point of view is used most in the stories, will have your role changed from chapter to chapter. Sometimes you are a "non-IT" person, other chapters a "Tech Support" person. Every story will start with your experience, perspective, and struggles. We will also be painting a complete picture. Every tale has two sides. While this is IT Hell, we will be looking at the backstory to help you fully understand why IT departments fall apart. Ultimately, we will help you understand that, yes, the IT Help Desk might truly hate talking to you too.

We will also introduce the "IT Hells." These are representations of the issues that lead to awful IT experiences and environments. These are depictions of the worst that a mismanaged, poorly funded, untrained, and disrespected IT department can foster.

These chapters are full of real stories with real people. We have changed the names, not to protect the innocent, as **no one is truly innocent of creating or facilitating IT hells.** We have changed their names to easier ones to remember so you and your team can discuss these stories and use them to improve your team.

Use these stories to have conversations with your team. If your name happens to get used in one of the stories and the actions of one of the **"IT Demons"** hits too close to home, too bad, you are part of the problem. You would not be reading this book if your IT team was perfect, and to be frank, no IT team is.

You are reading this book as one of three people:

1. The Non-IT person who has had it with their IT team and is looking for ways to improve it. You might be a leader in your organization or an employee looking for ways to improve the IT experience.

2. The IT person who is simply done. You are done being yelled at. Done with the long hours. Done with being overworked.

3. The IT Team Manager (or leader, supervisor, CIO, or whatever label your organization uses) who needs to find solutions to the unmanageable demands from your leaders and for the team that simply can't catch up.

All of us are one of these. Yes, even you. If you love your IT Help Desk team and think they do not need help or have no room for improvement, stop lying to yourself. These "unicorn" teams are a trap. They will promote all the competent employees into advanced roles, and the new crew will bring with them the hells and demons described here. **Turnover is ripe ground for demons to spawn** (See the chapter, "The Hell of Hiring, Training, and Firing").

You will find some harsh language in this book. If you are bothered by 'hell', 'dam,' 'shit,' or other '4-letter words,' this will be a tough read. As we said, these are real people with real reactions. When it comes to poor IT support, the reaction is always anger, and anger often lends itself to foul language.

We do not sugar coat ideas in this book. We are being direct and frank. **This is IT Hell, not IT Bad Place.**

There is a light at the end, however! Each scenario we present to you is avoidable and will not require massive amounts of money (usually) or firing (probably) and hiring (maybe) staff. We believe that **most** people want to succeed in their IT careers and overall expertise. We will lay forth guidelines, foundations, and sometimes, outright rules on improving your Help Desk team.

We will also introduce "**IT Saints**" (there are not many), IT employees who already embrace the ideals that keep their team out of IT Hell. Take advantage of these saints' desirable attributes that are helping to hold up your team. You will never have a "perfect" employee, but you can have fantastic ones who bring joy to everyone they interact with. We can work with these employees and use their passion to help battle the IT Hells.

We will use generalizations, lots of generalizations. We will demonstrate a scenario or a person, and you will say, "not me," or "not my team." These are the exceptions. If we say an "IT Pro is (blank)" or an "IT Team is (blank)," we mean that as a guiding principle because there are always exceptions. If we went after every possible example, this book would never end. In these stories presented, we will offer solutions to these hells and a path towards IT Heaven.

Each chapter will describe an "IT Hell." These are the realms of the IT Demons and the pits from which they spawn. Your organization will likely have multiple hells. Each hell spawns from the presence of these IT demons and their various mindsets, and in turn, the hells can create more demons, and these demons can foster new hells. Some chapters will only be full of stories, while others may be heavy on data with links to the sources. We will provide insight and strategies on how to pull your Help Desk team out of such hells.

This book also focuses on the Help Desk. While many of the ideas in this book can work for higher-level IT and non-IT teams (such as server administration or customer service), this book is focused entirely on front line end-user IT support. This book addresses the issues and hells of the face of the IT department, The Help Desk.

Now, on to the first hell.

The Hell of IT Expenditure

Welcome to our first hell, The Hell of IT Expenditure. This is the first hell because it is both the easiest to escape from and the least detrimental to an organization and its IT team. This hell can be managed with and even avoided by having strong IT leadership (see the chapter, "The Hell of Leadership"), hiring well (see the chapter, "The Hell of Hiring, Training, and Firing), and a robust IT Culture (see the chapter, "The Hell of Culture).

Corporation and organization leadership: this chapter is primarily for you. The IT department has come to you countless times for the money to upgrade a system or software, and you roll your eyes at the expense. But, there is a hard fact that every organization needs to adopt: **Every employee uses technology for every job and function**. The delivery driver uses IT to log their time. The company owner uses IT to pull reports and send emails. Outages and unstable connection affect productivity and, ultimately, the company's ability to make money; that is the true cost of not adequately investing in IT.

Say it with us: **IT is not an expense; it is an investment.** Say it again. IT leaders, frame your conversations with this mantra.

Not every "IT Demon" is an IT team member, though. The most common demon in corporate leadership is the **"Good Enough Gary."** This demon has usually never worked IT and loves to say, "What we have is working, so why change?" or "Things are good enough, so why spend more?" The more nefarious spawning of this demon is the Gary who once worked in IT. They have long left the technology world and frame their thoughts and perspectives from how IT was when they left IT years ago. Technology changes fast; according to Moore's law (Index 4 #9), technology can double in usage capability or half in cost every eighteen months. To combat a Gary, this demon must be presented with facts on the true cost of not spending money on IT infrastructure. Sometimes a

Hell Desk To Help Desk

catastrophic outage helps to vanquish this demon, but usually not. When the outage occurs, Gary will chastise IT for not "fixing it" or "supporting it" or simply "throwing money at it."

Follow along in this, our first story of **IT Hell**.

You are the IT manager. Your phone rings one night and wakes you up. It's the main warehouse.

Warehouse Manager: "Every printer just stopped, and we can't get the deliveries out."

You pull the phone away from your face and force your eyes to focus and read the time. It's 4:17 AM.

You: "Ok, let me call some people."

You hang up and call the IT on-call number. It goes to voicemail. While leaving a voicemail, you hear an incoming call beep. You finish leaving the message and see that the VP of Shipping has called. You call the VP back.

VP: "What the hell happened?"

You: "I don't know yet; I just got called by the warehouse. Getting my team spun up."

VP: "Get it fixed, now! Keep me on the line until we are back up and running."

You: "Sir, may I hang up so I can call them?"

VP: "You can put me on hold."

You place the VP on hold and start to call your team directly.

Steve: "Hey boss, what do you need?"

You: "Every printer stopped at Warehouse 1. Can you check the network and servers?"

Steve: "Yeah, let me see. Can I call you back?"

You: "Yes, please hurry."

You hang up and call your senior team member.

Nick: "It's 4:30; why are you calling?"

You: "Never mind Nick, big emergency. Warehouse 1 cannot print. Can you help?"

Nick: "Andy is on call."

You: "Nick, I really need some help. Please log in and check the servers. You know better than anyone."

Nick: "Gahh, fine, give me a minute."

You click back over to the still holding VP.

You: "Can we start a conference call with the warehouse?"

VP: "You tell me, you are IT. And just so you know, every minute we are down, we are losing 500 dollars."

You try to stifle a laugh. You recall sending a 'Request For Quote' for a messaging and phone system that handles this type of situation. Senior leadership did not see the value in paying $15 per user per year for this.

You: "I think my cell can handle a conference call. Let me call the warehouse and my team back."

You place the VP on hold and add the warehouse manager, Steve, and Nick, back to the call.

Hell Desk To Help Desk

You: "Hey Steve and Nick, any updates?"

Nick: "Yeah, I see the issue. The server host for the print server is down."

You: "Can we get it back up?"

Nick: "No, we have to restore from backup."

You: "When was the last backup, and how long to get it back up?"

Nick: "Yesterday at 5 pm, and someone has to drive in and restore from the tape, so 2 or 3 hours."

You hear the VP sputter.

VP: "3 hours!!!!! Do we have another printer server?"

You: "No, that request was denied as it was estimated to cost $15,000."

VP: "We lost that much money before I even called you!"

You: "Yeah, and any print jobs sent after 5 pm will need to be resent."

VP: "This is going to cost us thousands, plus the hundreds of pissed-off customers whose deliveries we will miss."

What led up to this? In this very real scenario, the host server was over ten years old, and the hard drive catastrophically crashed. The old server was not configured in any sort of internal redundancy as it was a repurposed server and not one designed for critical production systems. They did not have any monitoring or failover for the servers as the corporation relied on the "Scream Test" to monitor its systems. (as in; users will call and scream when something is broken). They were still using tape backups because they were deemed "good enough." There was no adequate communication and collaboration tool as it was considered too expensive to implement.
    Let's fast forward an hour and see how the recovery is going.

You pull into the parking lot at 5:01 am. Traffic was light as most of the world was asleep. You make your way into the IT office and are disappointed to find it empty. You asked your team to hurry over and begin the recovery.

At 5:26 AM, Steve rolls in. He is wearing shorts and the remnants of a breakfast burrito on his shirt.

You: "Can you start the recovery?"

Steve: "Maybe, I have never done it."

You: "Can you check the backup tape and make sure it's okay?"

Steve: "Sure, boss."

You call Nick. He sounds half asleep when he answers.

Nick: "What now?"

You: "I am going to assume you are almost here?"

Nick: "My shift is not until 9."

You: "We have a major outage. You need to come in."

Nick: "Andy is on call. He should be there."

You: "Steve is here; I have not heard from Andy yet. I need you; you know the servers best."

Nick: "Gahh, fine, but I want double comp time."

You: "Fine, just get here."

Nick: "Let me shower, eat, and drive over."

Hell Desk To Help Desk

You: "Can you skip the shower and breakfast?"

Nick: "Nope, don't want to get unhealthy."

You hang up in utter disbelief. *Where is Andy?*

You walk back to check on Steve.

You: "How does it look?"

Steve: "Well, I pulled the tape, and then two things happened?"

You: *Sigh*. "What now?"

Steve: "First, the label on the tape is from last week. No one has changed it since last Monday."

You: "Ok, did it at least grab last night's backup?"

Steve: "That was the other thing: when I pulled the tape, the server turned off, and I cannot turn it back on."

You: "The server is dead?"

Steve: "I think so."

You: "Do we have a spare that we can turn on?"

Steve: "No."

On the after-action, you find out that the tape had not been changed in six days. One of the consecutive backups maxed out the tape. The system saved the backup image on its internal storage since the tape was full. The internal storage quickly filled and caused the server to crash. In the past, an image of the server had a change made but not applied. After the crash, the backup taken that previous Monday was actually an image of the server from months prior. The image being overloaded broke it and required professional hard drive recovery to get some of the data back. Most from the last few months were lost. This is the most valuable of all business assets… customer data, gone. This crash ultimately led to the business losing so many customers that it was bought out by a larger company, with nearly all employees losing their jobs.

The right technology to prevent and remediate disasters is expensive, but it should not be viewed as an expense. It's a genuine investment, a potential lifesaver. This company needed to desperately upgrade its servers and set up some sort of redundancy. They needed to move from tape backups to a modern solution. They needed to purchase actual monitoring solutions. They needed to have a better communication solution than just cell phones.

These things can be costly, but not having them is overwhelmingly expensive. Too often, a business views IT as an expense. "We have to buy laptops again? We just did three years ago!" Sure, you can put it off and save some money upfront, but the hidden costs of time and repairs on the dated hardware are more than the replacement cost. A study by Microsoft found that not replacing your laptop actually costs almost $3,000 (Index 4 #1).

- The optimal age of PCs and hardware is no older than **4 years**, beyond which they are more expensive to maintain than replace.

- A PC that is 4+ years old is **2.7 times** more likely to be repaired, resulting in **112 hours** of productive time lost.

- The total cost of owning a 4+-year-old PC is **US$2,736,** enough to replace with two or more newer PCs!

This expense is true for servers and all other technology hardware, too (Source IDC, 2015).

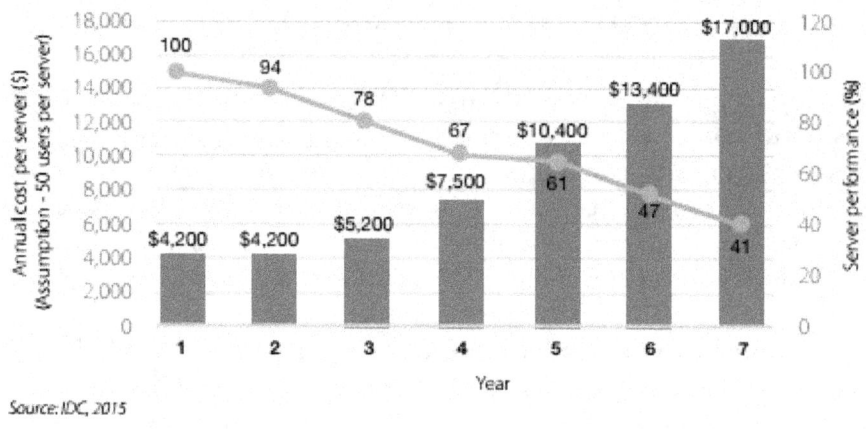

Every study shows the same thing: having sound architecture, modern backup solutions, and up-to-date fail-over environments always saves money. Beyond just saving money, proper IT investment improves the user experience.

IT software and hardware need to be viewed as depreciating capital. Just as you spend money on buildings, vehicles, and furniture, IT equipment should be considered to be a necessary investment in the stability and continued growth of your company: Computers are used by all of your employees, the dock loader uses a computer to record time and document what was unloaded, a janitor uses a computer to order supplies and control the HVAC, and the CEO uses a computer to view financial reports and check emails. Any unjustified cuts (i.e., to save money) will slow an employee's output and day-to-day capabilities and, in effect, reduce returns and productivity.

Software releases are developed at a breakneck pace. If your organization is not staying up to date, your users will not be able to communicate and collaborate effectively and efficiently with each other and with clients. Some companies attempt to circumvent this by under-buying licenses or illegally obtaining them.

We interviewed one leader who tells the story of a company they supported that had only five licenses for the current version of Microsoft Office, two for Acrobat, and only one for a specific design software suite. The dozens of other employees all used free or even illegal software. When specific files needed to be opened, printed, or converted, the IT team had to arrange a time and work as a "file conversion team" to help give users access to media.

Illegal software use is rampant and dangerous in the business world. While it may seem like a way to save money, it ultimately poses two risks (Index 4 #10):

1. Illegal software will often come from nefarious sources and bring viruses and other malware along with it.
2. If the government finds out, the fines can be as high as $15,000 per instance.

An honest and competent IT leader will hold firm in purchasing and paying for the proper licensure for the organization's needs. This protects the company from the legal and security risks involved in using "pirated" software (Read more in the chapter, "The Hell of IT Leadership"). The viruses that can come with illegally obtained software open up digital doors for a ransomware attack and data theft; these are billion-dollar industries whose only goal is to lock down and steal your data and sell it back to you at a premium. We cannot stress it enough; **only IT Demons use illegal software.**

Here is our list of IT systems that every **help desk** must have:

1. An Automated call/paging "On Call" system.
    a. There must be a way to control the calls and the frequency of calls to your agents.
    b. There must also be a way to track the number of calls and call patterns
    c. This system helps prevent abuse and ensures that proper escalation paths are followed.
2. A ticket system to track **ALL** IT work.
    a. Emails and notepad documents do not cut it and always get lost

b. You need reporting and metrics on the tickets, patterns, and flow.
   c. If it is not in a ticket, it did not happen.

3. Central storage of **ALL** IT knowledge
   a. This could be combined with the ticket system.
   b. All tasks done by your IT team does must be stored somewhere accessible; do not trust memories, shared documents, etc.
4. A system monitoring and alerting tool.
   a. When things break, you need to know that users calling for a problem is not the appropriate solution.

5. On-call phone(s).
   a. DO NOT GIVE OUT PERSONAL NUMBERS.
   b. Ideally, every agent on the rotation has a separate phone provided by the organization.

6. A customer service/employee recognition system.
   a. Tangible rewards for good performance (gift cards, TVs, cruises!)
   b. Positive customer feedback to drive performance.

These 6 tools are critical for an efficient help desk. If even one tool is missing, the team will struggle to succeed, allowing IT Demons to take hold and quickly unleash hell on your operation. If your IT Help Desk is large enough, have a phone tracking system to know the agent's status. Anything more than ten agents should have a system of this type. You need to know that someone is available to take calls from users. This only gets harder as teams grow in size.

IT expenditure is not limited to devices and software. The organization must be willing to spend sufficiently on education and hiring. Having an uneducated workforce will cost you both money and, more importantly, public opinion. Read more on this concept in the chapter, "The Hell of an Uneducated Employee." As to hiring, pay what the market demands, or slightly better. The chapter, "The Hell of Hiring, Training, and Firing," goes into depth on the importance of proper salaries.

Do not skimp on paying to train your IT agents. Their growth is key to the success of your Help Desk. Improving the skillsets of your current employees reduces downtime and increases speed to resolution, which reduces the cost to the company as a whole, and improves their customer service abilities (Read more on these concepts in the chapter, "The Hell of Hiring, Training, and Firing" and "The Hell of Impressions").

We can already hear the complaint from the Garys and other IT demons: "What about the cost!" Go back earlier in this chapter and read again about the true expense of not properly investing in IT systems. **Your IT leader must push and present the case for expenditure clearly, consistently, and competently.** It must be a regular conversation. Part of these conversations must also include the savings. Celebrate the wins of the money you save with contract negotiations, package purchases, and employee productivity improvement.

Approach leadership with the 'Return On Investment' (ROI) on all the purchased software and hardware. Get granular- add up the seconds, minutes, days, and hours the IT team has saved the company. Present these time savings in real dollar amounts. Present worst-case scenarios and the real-world savings that the proper IT equipment and software provide. The IT leader must work with each department and talk about the cost per minute/hour/day their team will face if they lose access to technology services. Use this data to build your presentation for your purchase requests.

All businesses are ultimately in the same business money. Speak to them in their language. There's no need to get overly technical. Simple phrases like, "This keeps the printers printing if a server crashes" (redundant servers), or, "This keeps the phones on during a power out" (battery backup), or, "This keeps the computers online if we lose internet" (cellular backup) are most effective. Once you state the reason, say the savings as such:

"The cost of a backup server is (insert current market price). The time to restore the server under the best-case scenario is (insert your current backup procedure estimate time to recovery). A single server outage will cost roughly (insert the cost of the downtime) while we recover."

Lastly, **IT Leaders should not use this chapter as a weapon against the company leadership.** There is the truth that you can overbuild. You need to know your end-user demand and plan for growth. Do not buy a firewall that can handle 5000 VPN connections if you only have 200 employees in the company. Conversely, do not buy a 200 connection VPN only to purchase a larger one in the near future. Present to the company leadership clear usage expectations, including estimates for any increase over the next three years (product life cycle), and present them with the best fit for your needs. **Do not overbuy!** You must build that relationship of trust and show skills and knowledge in presenting proper expenditures. Leadership needs to view the IT leader as knowledgeable, but more importantly, trustworthy.

We understand the temptation to purchase the "best" and "shiniest" equipment, but IT Demons are selfish creatures who want all the shiny new hotness. You must fight this temptation and their demands, as it is a sin that can lead to IT Hell. This takes us directly to our next hell.

The Hell of Impressions

You are a customer service manager working on a presentation. You want to ensure that your laptop will work with the projector in the meeting room, but you dread what has to happen next: you have to talk to IT. You pick up your desk phone and dial the Help Desk number. No surprise, it goes to voicemail. The meeting is in an hour, and you want to make sure everything goes over smoothly, so you pick up your laptop and walk down to take the elevator to subfloor 1, the IT team's domain.

You can hear the IT room from down the hall. There is music streaming, and two guys argue which is better, XBOX or PlayStation. You walk the darkened hall towards the noise. You reach the door and examine it. The door has the "Technology" corporate sign, but also on the door are stickers for Linux, EMC, and Cisco placed in a random arrangement. The mailbox next to the door is overflowing with employee notes asking for support and mail from various IT vendors.

You knock on the door. No one answers. You are sure they can't hear you over the music. You open the door, and the smells of old tacos and spilled energy drinks overwhelm you. You survey the mess. To your right is a workbench covered in computer parts, and tools are strewn about. The walls are adorned with creased Star Wars posters and various toys. The garbage cans are overflowing with junk food wrappers. The two guys arguing over video game consoles are at the rear of the room, and they do not look up to greet you when you enter. To your left, the desk by the door is empty. The phone on the desk starts to ring, another user desperate for help.

You clear your throat, "Excuse me," you say over the music to the two guys arguing, "can I get some help, please?"

The bald, skinny one on the right answers, "Steve went to poo, he will be right back."

"Can either of you help?" you ask.

The one on the left responds, "Nope. We are not Help Desk. Steve is Help Desk."

You recognize his voice, "Are you, Nick?"

Nick does not hide his frustration at his day being interrupted, "Why?"

"You helped me a few weeks ago," you say. "Can you help me today?"

"No," he says with exasperation, "I am not Help Desk today- Steve is Help Desk this week."

From the back of the room, you hear a toilet flush. Steve bursts in from the back.

He exited the bathroom way too quickly to have washed his hands.

"Woo!" Steve yells, "That bathroom is toast. Stay out for at least an hour."

You watch Steve saunter to the fridge and pull out an energy drink. His *My Little Pony* shirt has a hole on the back and does not fully cover his rotund belly in the front. Some shredded cheese is clinging to his collar. He is wearing grey sweatpants and camouflage crocs. His hair is uncombed, and he hasn't shaved in weeks. He pops open the energy drink and gulps it down in one swig. He burps loudly and tosses the can at the trash can, which ultimately bounces off the side and rattles on the concrete floor. Steve looks up and makes eye contact with you.

He lets out an audible sigh. He grabs a bag of chips from a box on top of the fridge, opens it, and pops a chip in his mouth.

"Steve, are you Steve?" you roar over the music. "Can you help me?"

Steve sighs again. He slimes over to his desk and falls into his chair in a grunt.

"Hold on," he says, "boss says first come, first served."

You look around, confused and irritated, for the imaginary person who was there before you.

Steve picks up the phone and starts checking voicemails. You watch him as he deletes messages without writing anything down. He hangs up the phone and turns to his computer.

"My turn?" you ask.

"Nope," replies Steve with a burp, "emails."

From the entrance, IT Manager walks in. He is wearing a tank top, running shorts, and sneakers. He is sweaty and breathing hard.

"That was a solid run," he announces to the room. "How was lunch, fellas?"

The manager does not even acknowledge you.

Nick replies, "We had Mexican at that new place on Main Street. Steve just wrecked the bathroom, so hold off on your shower."

"I don't have a choice," says the manager as he heads to the back, "I got a vendor buying me drinks in an hour."

"Can I get some help?" you call after the manager.
"Talk to Steve; he is Help Desk," he calls back without even looking at you as he disappears into the bathroom.

Hell Desk To Help Desk

You storm out. As the door closes behind you, you can hear laughter and inappropriate comments.

Sound familiar? How many IT teams conduct themselves like this? "Not my IT team," you say to yourself. Sure, your team may not be the total Hell pictured here. But, be honest with yourself. Parts of this story bring back memories.

This is our 2nd Hell, **The Hell of Impressions.** This is another Hell that can be managed or worked through with sound leadership and a positive IT culture.

We have all met a 'not my job Nick' or a 'sloppy Steve.' How many IT Rooms are more dorm rooms and less like professional offices? How many IT managers are too focused on the corporate side and promotion and not on the face of IT, the Help Desk?

How do we change the perception of IT in our organization?

It starts with culture and buy-in from the whole team. Everyone must take part. When a user interacts with the Help Desk, that is their entire perception of the entire IT organization. One bad interaction can wreck a user's trust and respect for years. Read more of this mindset in the chapter, "The Hell of Culture."

Users are twelve times more likely to share a negative IT experience than a positive one. This means that whenever there is an interaction with a 'Not My Job Nick' refusing to help or a 'Sloppy Steve' spilling an energy drink on a user's desk, your team has to be awesome twelve times over just to recover and get back to tolerance.

Where do we start to improve the organizational perception of the IT team? With first impressions. Visualize in your mind a state-of-the-art, high-tech IT office. What do you see?

Most visualize clear, spotless glass desks and doors with stainless steel frames and glass cabinets holding rows of servers that are humming along happily as little green and blue lights constantly flicker.

Now, imagine the ideal technician. For many of you, the visual is as follows:

The technician walking the aisle is wearing clean, pressed, dark pants. His white long-sleeve button-up is almost angelic. His sleeves are rolled up to expose his wrists, signaling that he is simultaneously fashion-forward and hardworking. His tie matches his belt and shoes. He is clean-shaven with neatly combed hair held in place with the appropriate amount of gel. He is fit and handsome, and he smiles and greets people who pass by. He pauses by a server, taps the touchscreen in his hand, and then nods at the results. He oozes confidence, and his whole appearance is welcoming.

Do you employ this tech? Probably not. So few techs will be a 'Perfect Patrick.' Why is that? What is this fictional employee doing that yours are not? Nothing in our visualization was about his skill. He was simply a well-dressed, handsome, friendly fellow. He walked the hall with a warm, career-oriented disposition, appearing to know how to do his job with skill and genuine personal interest.

That last part is the key. We will call it, "Give-A-Shitness." Does your team appear to give a shit? Do they care not only about the technology but also about the perception of the IT team and relationships with the greater organization? If you say you care, do you project that care into your everyday actions and appearance?

IT team leaders: do you have tough conversations with your colleagues about presentation and first impressions? Do you have set guidelines for professionalism and cleanliness? We are not saying to require slacks and ties or dresses. We are saying to set standards with your team so, at a minimum, they can blend in around the corporate office. If the corporate standard is polo shirts and slacks, that should be your baseline. If the corporate standard is a t-shirt and jeans, match it. As a leader, make it your mission to support this and provide clear expectations. At the least, your IT team should be able to walk the halls and pass for an employee of the organization. Provide your team with the shirts you deem appropriate and model their wearing. Read more on branding your team and its benefits in the chapter, "The Hell of Culture."

Hell Desk To Help Desk

Individuals working in IT: how much thought do you put into your appearance, the cleanliness of your workspace, and your interactions with the employee's organization or the users you assist? **It is a hard truth, but the world will judge you by your appearance and ability to interact with and relate to others.** How do you want your first impression to be received? We are not saying wear a tie or a nice dress every day. We do recommend at least trying dressing up once in a while and see how your interactions improve.

Here are our "5 Rules for IT Dress Code." These are simple guidelines that all IT teams should aim to adopt.

1. Never, ever wear sweatpants, jogging shirts, yoga pants, torn jeans, bathing suits, sleeveless shirts, mid-drifts, flip-flops, crocs, or anything you would wear to a beach, gym, or pool.

2. Only wear shorts and sleeveless shirts when doing out-of-office work in the heat, such as running cables outdoors.

3. Never be in the office dressed down. We encourage working out but make sure to shower and change before going back to the office. If the shower is in the office, be discreet with your post-gym return.

4. Daily: shower, brush your teeth, comb/brush your hair, and wear a clean shirt.

5. Polo shirts or button-up shirts are some of the basics- the more professional you look, the more professional you will feel and act.

What do you see not in our rules? Any mention of tattoos, beards, piercings, or hairstyle/color. We encourage these lifestyle things. Your IT department should be unique and fun and have a personality all of its own. As long as your team stays within the corporate guidelines, and follows our five rules, encourage them to express themselves. Have fun with this: have the team dress up on holidays and special events. If the organization has a Halloween costume contest, encourage your team to participate. Have an annual "fancy dinner" and pay for the team to bring a date and dress up. These types of events promote relationships, community, and pride across the organization. Read more in the chapter, "The Hell of Culture."

You will be blown away by the changes in professionalism you will see when your team "dresses the part." We see it time and time again. When someone dresses professionally, they feel and act professionally.

Now that the team is looking sharp, how about the office?

When we described the office, did it seem too familiar? What is it with IT rooms being messy? Why do they have stickers and posters all over the place? And what is with the toys? Other departments can stay clean and be presentable, so why not IT?

This starts with an idea that must be first understood:

IT Professionals are unique outside of the reality of all others.

Sorry salespeople, IT professionals are the most unique. IT pros are the "nerds among nerds." **While many will simply use a computer to complete work, these nerds choose to work on computers**. They are think first and sometimes think only people. More personal activities like cleaning, organizing the office, and being social can be outside their realm. These are often individuals who find comfort in video games, fantasy worlds, and dark rooms. It is not that they don't care, but more that they genuinely don't see the problem sometimes.

The IT Demon who lives in this realm is **"Sloppy Steve."** This is the most typical visual of IT stereotypes. The morbidly obese, Cheetos-stained shirt wearing, neck-bearded, non-showered, rude, impatient slob. The guy who makes a noise every time he stands up. The guy who is always eating and leaving his food remnants everywhere. The tech who is constantly losing his tools and never cleaning up his workbench. He is why the janitor refuses to enter the IT room to empty the trash cans.

If a tech does not present themselves well, can they also be expected to have a presentable workspace and thought-out interactions with users? We are not saying that every tech needs to be physically fit, well dressed, and attractive.

Hell Desk To Help Desk

However, we are saying that there are minimal standards of presentation and hygiene that should be expected of your staff. When hiring, there are signs to look for to avoid onboarding a "Sloppy Steve." You can also have conversations and techniques available when you have already hired a Steve and need to rectify.

We will cover more of the signs to look for during a hiring interview in the chapter, "The Hell Of Hiring, Firing, and Training" to avoid a "Sloppy Steve." This chapter is about how to help course correct and convert a Steve from a demon to a saint. The first step is to go back earlier in this chapter and re-read the "5 Rules for IT Dress Code." Have the IT Manager lead a team huddle and talk about each rule with your team. Do not single out any individuals, and do not let the IT team signal any of them out. Make the "5 Rules For IT Dress Code" an agreed contract with your team. If needed, adjust to match your originations guidelines. If your organization requires shirts, ties, and dresses, talk this over with your IT team. Help them to see the perspective of the users. Ask them questions like, "if you went to a barber and they had dirty hands, would you want them touching your head and face?" Once the team has buy-in, enforce it. Start with private conversations with team members when they fail to meet the standard. These must be gentle conversations. Get their story. Find out what difficulties they have with meeting the standard. Most importantly, the IT manager must set the example and follow the rules, see the chapter "The Hell of Leadership."

Once the team is presentable, we are ready to move on to the office.

The reality of modern IT support is this: IT Support professionals must work dozens of types of tasks every day, as quickly as possible, while dozens of other people are screaming for help. Their work is unpredictable and varies widely from user to user. IT professionals work with users who lie and hide their computer usage out of embarrassment, complicating the work further. IT professionals usually work non-stop from open to close and simply do not have time to tidy up. They are interrupted all day with phone calls, emails, and people barging into their space because each person's situation is "catastrophic to the entire business if not fixed immediately." By the time the last person leaves the building, IT support employees are burned out and want nothing more than to go home and relax. Your IT team simply does not have the time to support all users and keep clean (read more on making this time in the chapter, "The Hell of Expectations").

Other teams and fields of work more easily have a singular and clearly defined goal. Marketing produces media, sales creates and fulfills orders, janitorial cleans the buildings, supply chain delivers the product, and the corporate leadership team provides guidance. Each of these teams are supported by the IT team, making each team's IT needs unique and of higher importance than anyone else. **While most teams only have one group they answer to, IT answers to all groups.**

Your IT team needs time to put away their tools, straighten up, and the luxury of being able to simply come up for air. It is human nature to socialize and seek enjoyment. If your IT team is not afforded this time, they will find it at the expense of the business's unmet needs. We dive deeper into this in the chapter, "The Hell Of Expectations". The takeaway, for now, is that we must allocate time during the workweek for the IT team to make its office presentable and be able to step away from work to relax. This time must be well-published and agreed upon with the organization. Just like a teacher has a planning period or a public pool has an "adult swim" time, the IT teams need the "kids out of the pool" time to clean up and catch their breath.

Once we have time to organize, we would need to plan the layout of the IT room because there should be defined workspaces for specific tasks. If your IT team supports server builds, have a specific area with the proper tools. Food and break areas should be separate from the work area (read more in the chapter, "The Hell of IT Culture"). Have assigned desks for each agent, which is more than just a health and sanitation concern. Agents will adopt a sense of ownership over their desks, and encourage fellow coworkers to do the same. The agents will begin to take pride in the presentation of their office (read more on this in the chapter, "The Hell of Culture").

Aside from an organized and clean office and the required equipment, we offer these:

Hell Desk To Help Desk

5 Rules for What Goes in the IT Office:

1. Decorations should align with the business as a whole and presented tastefully.

2. No food, only water.

3. Music should be played via headsets. Hold non-work conversations while users are being serviced.

4. No personal tools.

5. Family photos are encouraged.

At first glance, these may seem harsh, but let's break down the reasons behind each of these.

Decorations should align with the business as a whole and be presented tastefully. We are not saying not to have pop-culture posters, toys, or stickers. However, we advise you to make your public space presentable and enjoyable. When users come in, we want them to feel welcome and at ease, not overwhelmed and discombobulated. If we have sloppy doors covered with stickers askew and cluttered walls covered with ripped and slanted posters, the users enter the room already negatively perceiving IT and the Help Desk agents.

On the other hand, if decorations are neat and respectable, they can be great conversation starters and help break the ice with users who enter already in foul moods. Most people enjoy pop culture. They may not wear costumes to Comic-Con, but that does not mean they don't enjoy the movies. While those in IT tend to stay attached to toys and video games, most users did enjoy them 'once upon a time.'

Having a professionally appealing office encourages professional behaviors from your team. If it looks like a frat house, expect that behavior. If it looks and feels like a professional environment, expect the team to treat it as such.

No food, only water. This may be a hard one for your team. They are addicted to their energy drinks, and they are so far behind that they "have to eat lunch at their computer." IT professionals tend to be more anti-social, so they often have little desire to go out for lunch. However, the research is clear: having dedicated time away from your work for breaks and meals increases overall productivity and produces far greater results than employees who work through breaks and during meals. This is where leadership needs to set the example and enforce the behavior. Encourage breaks away from the office and work. (read more in the chapter, "The Hell of Culture"). Off-set break times so one team member can still answer phones and not have the minor hell of an "unmanned IT office."

IT equipment is expensive, sensitive, and fragile. Sugary drinks are the bane of any circuit board they encounter. Food particles and smelly food wrappers only distract from the work and create more giant messes that attract pests. The end-user will not take your team seriously if they are too distracted by overwhelming odors and the sight of a tech eating a Hot-Pocket at their computer. You can help enforce this behavior by purchasing the team water bottles with your IT Department's logo. Read more about this in the chapter, "The Hell of Culture."

Music should be played via headsets. Hold non-work conversations while users are being serviced. We are not saying "no music allowed." We are saying that the user gets priority. They deserve the IT agent's undivided attention and clear lines of communication. If you are programming, building, or doing any work that does not require user interaction, headsets are acceptable and encouraged. As for conversations, no one is saying that the team can't joke around and have fun while working. What we are suggesting, however, is to set professional boundaries by holding all non-work conversations until end users have left the room and phone conversations are concluded. You also may not fully realize who is on the phone and how clearly they hear you. There is little more damning to a team's reputation than to hear the IT team gossiping about another employee.

From the user's perspective, if they are on the phone and hear music, talking, and laughing in the background, they perceive the IT team as amateur and uncommitted to the company's success. This may not be true, but it is the user's perspective, and with that perspective, they will share it with others. This creates a poor perception with the organization that the IT team is just "goofing off," leading to most IT problems. If the organization believes that the IT team is professional and has the organization's best interest driving their actions, users will demonstrate greater patience with the team when outages and other problems occur.

No personal tools. "But, but, I have my super, mega, deluxe lifetime warranty battery-powered multi-tool that I must use." Personal tools get borrowed and lent and are often returned broken, or not even at all. This creates conflicts between agents that we do not see with work-provided tools. Have the team's tools in marked designated areas. The team will hold each other accountable for returning the tools they all need and use. Purchase all the tools your team needs to succeed. Do not cut corners on IT expenses. Read more of this in the chapter, "Hell IT Expenditure."

Once your team has a professional-grade and fully-equipped set of tools, they will treat them like professional-grade tools. The behavior change is evident when using a matching, beautiful, complete set. The team leader will have to do some modeling and enforcing of the appropriate treatment of the tools, but the shift towards a more organized office will be quick. If an agent is abusive of the devices in any way, treat the event as it is in reality: vandalism or theft.

Family photos are encouraged. This is not limited to people. Photos can be of pets, cars, guitars, boats, or anything personal. Like decorations, these are conversation starters and help create connections and relationships between the techs and the users. This is different from shared decorations as they are more specific for each tech. Encouraging personalization goes beyond pop culture references and brings relatability into the tech environment.

We heard a story of a senior leader learning about an agent who liked to fish and had a boat. This leader invited himself over, which eventually led to the leader becoming an outspoken advocate of the IT Department.

You want your users and techs to have personal connections. When they have an emotional attachment to one another, the techs are no longer just boring techs, and users are no longer faceless demanders. They start to become something more, and they might just even become friends!

Your team is going to fight these rules. All demons fight exorcism. These need to be conversations that are direct and open. Approach your team as an ally and work with them to better understand how impressions affect their relationships with users. The leader must be the first to adopt these ideas, as the team will not surpass the level set by their leader.

This is going to be difficult. Some of your agents are going to feel personally attacked. Some may quit, and some may react in such an intensely negative way that it will require Human Resources intervention. We are not recommending replacing employees over dress code or messy workspace. We are saying, though, that if an employee cares so little about basic hygiene and appearance, how much will they care about user issues? Train your employees on these standards, educate them on why they are helpful, and create an advantage when working with users.

With that, on you go to our next hell.

The Hell of an Uneducated Employee

You are the Help Desk on-call this weekend. You have been fielding non-stop when Isaac, one of the longest-tenured employees, calls into the Help Desk to find a missing file. You are a little irritable as these calls are digging into your weekend relaxation time.

You: "Helpdesk here."

Isaac: "Hello, when I try to open a folder, I get an error."

You: "What error are you getting?"

Isaac: "File not found."

You: "Are you on the VPN?"

Isaac: "The what?"

You: "The virtual private network, are you on that?"

Isaac: "I am on the Wi-Fi."

Hell Desk To Help Desk

You: "Are you in the office or at home?"

Isaac: "Neither, I am at a coffee shop."

You: "Are you using the coffee shop's Wi-Fi?"

Isaac: "I think so; I can get on the internet."

You: "Ok, you need to use the VPN to get your files."

Isaac: "I've never had to use that before. They are on my laptop, I just need them to open."

You: "You need the VPN too. Can you please just turn it on?"

Isaac: "I don't think that is it. The folder is just not opening, but I can see it."

You: "That is a shortcut; it needs the VPN."

Isaac: "It's not a shortcut; it's a folder."

You: "It is a shortcut to a folder."

Isaac: "Shortcuts have a little arrow. This has a little red x."

You: "Because it needs the VPN."

Isaac: "My shortcut to the internet works."

You: "The internet does not need the VPN."

Isaac: "I did not need the VPN yesterday."

You: "Were you in the office yesterday?"

Isaac: "Why?"

You: "Why what?"

Isaac: "Why does it matter?"

You: "Why does what matter?"

Isaac: "Why does it matter if I was in the office yesterday?"

You: "If you are in the office, you do not need the VPN. If you are not in the office, you do."

Isaac: "That does not make sense."

You: "VPNs do not make sense?"

Isaac: "Why would I need something out of the office?"

You: "The VPN makes your computer think it is in the office."

Isaac: "So now the computer cares where it is?"

You: "Well, uh, for the files, it does."

Isaac: "How does a computer care?"

You: "It doesn't; it just needs to think it is in the office for the files to work."

Isaac: "We need to trick the computer?"

You: "No, the VPN puts the computer in the office."

Isaac: "I turn on the VPN, and the computer is in the office?"

You: "Yes."

Isaac: "I do not believe you. I am at a coffee house. There is no way the VPN moves my laptop to the office."

Hell Desk To Help Desk

You: "Ok, can we just try it?"

Isaac: "Ha, is this a trick? Are you trying to hack me?"

You: "You called me sir."

Isaac: "Oh yeah, I need my files. How can we recover them?"

You: "They do not need to be recovered, your computer just needs the VPN connected."

Isaac: "I need to be in the office to work? What is the point of a laptop?!?"

Ok, stop laughing; we know it's hard to read with a straight face. This conversation goes on for another hour. This was hell for both the tech and the employee. How can an educated employee whose entire profession relies on access to technology be so functionally illiterate about the technology he uses regularly? Time to meet another IT Demon, a non-IT demon. **Ignorant Isaac**. This is an educated adult professional who is either willfully or brazenly ignorant of IT. They not only do not understand IT, and if you attempt to help them with education or training, they can become hostile and take offense that you "dare to assume they are stupid."

Thus, the face of the matter is that your employees can be violently stupid regarding IT concepts. This ignorance is the largest source of call volume to the Help Desk and the single largest IT security risk.

This problem is widespread. It goes as high as the US government (hold on, lots of data is coming!)!

A Forbes article (Index 4 #2) highlights high-ranking US officials making outright stupid remarks about technology. I am sure you have heard how former first lady and former Secretary of State Hillary Clinton was asked about wiping her email server, and she responded with, "You mean with a towel?" Or the time the founder of Facebook, Mark Zuckerberg, was brought before congress and the hilarity of the truly foolish questions asked of him. Our personal favorite moment is when he explains the internet to Congress (see the transcript at Index 4 #11).

The United States Government ranks 24th in "IT Savvy" (Index 4 #3). This is pathetic. We should be #1, lightyears ahead of everyone else. As a country, the United States dominates all digital trends, culture shifts, and innovations. Why are the leaders of the US so uneducated, and to be honest, stupid about IT? Highly trained, educated, and experienced corporate leaders are not immune to looking foolish, too (Index 4 #4).

Technology ignorance is getting worse every day. It is genuinely scary when the most significant gap in IT security is the end-user and their education (Index 4 #5). Phishing campaigns, files being held hostage, and stolen data are costing users nearly $9 million a year (Index 4 #12). IT data hijacking is a big market, and it's ever-growing.

Technology improves at a breakneck pace, and with each innovation, the lack of general knowledge of how IT works decreases. With this decrease in understanding, the overall trust also dwindles (Index 4 #6). Users get comfortable with their technology, and as it improves, they become resistant to new electronics as the old was simply "good enough" (thanks, Gary!).

OK, enough data, you get it. People are offensively ignorant about technology.

How do we get our organization out of this hell? The IT Department needs to do more than just release, develop, and care for technology. Your IT team needs to have the **"heart of a teacher."** The IT team must aggressively and actively promote "Tier 0" support. Tier 0 is where end-users become more comfortable with and educated about technology to be able to solve their own simple issues eventually. We are not saying that your day-to-day employees need to know how to replace ram on a laptop or install software, but what we are saying is to assist them with understanding the **why** of the technologies you utilize and some basic self-support techniques.

Educate your users on what to expect and have available when calling the Help Desk. Self-completing a few simple tasks and having some basic information ready for the Help Desk agent will help make the call easier and quicker.

We made a universal list of Five things to do before calling the Help Desk:

1. Save all work.
2. Reboot your computer and try again.
3. Check with your team to see if the issue affects more than just you.
4. Take note of all the things you had open, and be ready to be fully honest about what you were doing when the issue started.
5. Take a deep breath and smile. The Help Desk wants to help. They are human, too, so treat them as such.

You may have more steps you require for your specific team, but these can get you started. Communicate and educate these requirements to your users. How each of these steps helps both the user and Help Desk Teams:

Save all work. This is a safety measure because we want to minimize all data and work loss. You should be saving frequently, but as soon as a user sees an issue, save and stop working to prevent further issues or complicate the current problem. If you can't save, do not close any applications.

Reboot your computer and try again. You would be shocked how often a simple reboot fixes the most common IT issues (Index 4 #13). The exception is if a reboot risks data loss or you want the Help Desk to see what is on your screen. If the user is able, it is ideal to take a screenshot before the reboot. If your computer is not in a working state to take a screenshot, or you do not know how, you can take a picture of the computer screen with your cell phone.

Check with your team to see if the issue affects more than just you. Often, IT issues that require a phone call affect more than just you. If your entire team calls in and bogs down the Help Desk phone lines, it will further delay helping users who are calling for a separate issue. If the entire team is affected, the IT team will usually only need one of you to call. A good IT team will have already identified the issue and was or will be communicating out what is going on (See the chapter, "The Hell of Expectations").

Take note of all the things you had open, and be ready to be fully honest about what you were doing when the issue started. A good Help Desk agent will ask these questions in their search for the root cause of your problem. Having this information accessible will assist the agent and expedite their process to resolve your issue. Also, be honest with the agent; if you were doing non-work activities (we all do it), tell the agent upfront about what website and applications (games) you had open. Unless the organization requires it, Help Desk agents are pretty good about keeping your secrets (*WINK*). Besides, we know what websites you browse and the applications you use. After all, it's part of our job (see the chapter, "The Hell of Culture").

Take a deep breath and smile. The Help Desk wants to help. They are human, too, so treat them as such. Your IT team wants to help. Really, they do. Remember, they are human, too, individuals who wish to be treated with kindness, dignity, and respect. If you are kind and patient with the agent, a good agent will act the same. If you are angry and foul-mouthed, the agent will not only be less inclined to assist, but this is technically bullying and should never be tolerated (see the chapter, "The Hell of Expectations").

The IT team must also be training partners for the organization, helping employees improve their "tech-savvy" at every stage of their employment. We encourage IT teams to be engaged in employee onboarding, development, and education. Hosting training sessions has tremendous benefits for IT teams and organizations. Host "technology boot camps" on the simple actions employees can do to care for their own IT needs. When a user can self-resolve in the industry, we call this Tier 0 support. It is the fastest and cheapest of all support tiers.

Tasks non-IT employees should be able to handle:
- Loading paper into a printer
- Loading ink/toner into a printer
- Resetting their own password
- Plugging in a keyboard or mouse

Tasks non-IT employees should never be expected to handle:
- Replacing internal computer parts

- Installing software
- Setting up monitors/docking stations
- Moving equipment

In the above story, a simple understanding of VPN and network file shares would have prevented the call entirely. We want to compel organizations to invest in educating their staff on how to use the technologies and the *why and how* behind them. This catalyst for change must come from the IT Department and its leadership. They should be offering regularly-scheduled training and workshops at multiple levels. **The organization should view the IT Department as a training department.** We go over this more in the chapter called "The Hell of Culture."

With these self-support expectations, we want to stress one that we specifically see lacking in most organizations: They allow users to install their own software. This book is not about IT security, so we won't get too deep into this. **However, we will say that more IT problems are created by users self-installing software than are avoided.** Lock down the user's machines and govern what is on them.

IT needs to partner with your organizations and make learning fun. Here are some corporate engagements we have seen produce tremendous results:

1. Host a "lunch and learn" (*have the organization pay for the food!*).

2. Offer "Technology Bootcamps" for employees so they can expand their skill sets.

3. Provide "ride-alongs" where non-IT professionals work side-by-side with the IT agents and vice-versa.

4. Have the IT team train new hires on the technology they will use.

Host a "lunch and learn." These are fun events that create a casual atmosphere where IT and non-IT employees can engage and interact. Spoiler alert: offering free food will always attract an audience. Use these times to share what the IT team does and how they function with other departments. When releasing new software or technologies, use these sessions to educate and ease the users into the newest available features and how they will make their lives better. These sessions are also a great time to get feedback from the users on improving further IT service offerings. These sessions also empower your Help Desk agents as they are the ones to lead them (see the chapter, "The Hell of Culture").

Offer "Technology Bootcamps" for employees so they can expand their skill sets. As the name implies, these are sessions for better general technology skills. Your IT leader should work with the organization, look at the call volume and sources of tickets, and send out surveys to determine relevant boot camp topics (see the chapter, "The Hell of Leadership"); they can be simple boot camps like 'tips and tricks for Excel" or, "email rules and how to use them." They could even be more advanced, focusing on coding or desktop troubleshooting. Feel out how the organization responds and adjust to meet their demands. If no one in your organization uses a specific piece of software, don't offer training on it (see the chapter, "The Hell of IT Expenditure").

Provide "ride-alongs" where non-IT professionals work side-by-side with the IT agents and vice-versa. We had one leader tell us how all he did his first week at a new organization was sit next to salespersons and listen to them take calls. He got to know their entire lives before he even touched a computer. Not only did this give the IT leader a greater perspective on the flow of the business, but the business leaders were greatly impressed by his desire to learn and truly improve the business as a whole. These ride-alongs provide great exposure and real-life learning environments. Often, IT professionals will not truly understand what is on the other end of that call, so we encourage this to be part of the IT onboarding experience (see the chapter, "The Hell of Firing, Training, and Firing"). Having non-IT employees sit at the Help Desk can also be eye-opening. One leader at a Managed Service Provider (MSP) would invite the leaders of the business they serviced to come and spend the day in their "bullpen" (their Help Desk room). These leaders witness first-hand the rate at which calls come in and all that the agents have to do to assist each user. It clarified why there were delays in the phones being answered at times and why the agents would need so much time to research an issue.

Hell Desk To Help Desk

Have the IT team train new hires on the technology they will use. Much like the other points, this helps create a more personal relationship between users and the Help Desk. Having a Help Desk agent introduce technology to new hires ensures that their first connection is positive. Far too often, new employees' first Help Desk call is because something is broken. Training the employees also reduces future calls. When you have a class of new hires, and they are all logging into their computers for the first time, a Help Desk agent is already in the room to help address any possible issues on-site. This also allows the IT team to learn more about the pains of the onboarding process to, in turn, find ways to improve that experience (see the chapter, "The Hell of Culture").

Lastly, on education, we want to say this, "Help me, help you!" Depending on your level of IT reliance, over 15% of all support calls are education-based. **Investing in the education of your employees will reduce IT expenses and increase employee productivity.** Work with the organization by helping them understand IT's true cost vs. potential expense. Help them become comfortable and confident with their technology. Set self-support expectations for users so they have a firm understanding of what they can do themselves, what is an emergency, and what can wait from expectations set by IT leadership (see the chapter, "The Hell of IT Leadership").

This "setting of expectations" takes us to our next hell.

The Hell of Expectations

You are an advanced IT support agent working late to upgrade the email server. The upgrade is months past due, and you chance putting the company at a security risk if you wait any longer. You decided to do the work at 11 pm, thinking no one would notice the server being down for a reboot. You have been begging the leader to do this for weeks now, and they are finally permitting it tonight since you are on-call anyways. You do not have a test environment, so you simply run the upgrade and wish for the best.

You start the installation process and watch as the services go down. The installation starts trudging along and gives an estimated time to finish of three hours.

You sigh to yourself, "Guess I can grab a few z's." You set an alarm for 3 am to check on the server.

You are woken up less than an hour later by the on-call phone.

You: "Hello?"

Rita: "I can't get to my emails."

You: "What?"

Hell Desk To Help Desk

Rita: "I CAN'T GET TO MY EMAILS!!!!"

You: "Oh sorry, yes, the server is being upgraded."

Rita: "Stop it now and get me in."

You: "I can't, it will be down until 3 am."

Rita: "Not good enough."

She hangs up. You fall back asleep only to be woken up in thirty minutes by your phone. It's your boss.

IT Manager: "We need the email server back up."

You: "I can't, it's in the middle of an update. If we stop it, it will break."

IT Manager: "Why?"

You: "Why what?"

IT Manager: "Why is it updating?"

You: "It is way past due."

IT Manager: "Why tonight?"

You: "You told me to. You said that I was on-call and to go ahead and update the email server tonight."

IT Manager: "I did not mean bring it down."

You: "This update required the downtime. I told you this."

IT Manager: "You never told me this, at least not to this extent. Rita wants her email. She says she works late, and this messed up her routine."

You: "I'm sorry, but we're committed. It has already started, and stopping it now will break it. We have to wait."

IT Manager: "Can you hurry it along?"

You: "No."

IT Manager: "When will it be done?"

You: "3 am, maybe later. I still have to run some post-upgrade checks too."

IT Manager: "Rita wants a call every 15 minutes on progress. Call her every 15 minutes."

You: "You want me to call her every 15 minutes and say, 'Still going?'"

IT Manager: "Yes."

You: "Nothing will change until 3 am."

IT Manager: "I do not care, that is what she wants, and I am ordering you to do it."

You: "Can you convince her otherwise? Nothing is going to change for at least 3 hours."

IT Manager: "You can try and ask her at your next check-in call in fifteen minutes."

The phone clicks silent.

I hate my job.

Allow us to introduce our next IT Demon, "**Right-now Rita.**" This could be an IT or a non-IT employee. This is an individual who expects all IT solutions to be instant and their demands met. They want it "done yesterday!" All outages personally affect them and cost the organization "millions of dollars!"

These demons are born from an IT department that does not properly communicate and set expectations with their greater organization.

Say that phrase out loud, "**Set Expectations**." Repeat it again…. and again.

Your IT team must adopt this mantra. This idea must be in every interaction, every communication, and every meeting. This idea must permeate every IT employee and their entire communication framework. "Set Expectations."

Here are some examples:

1. A user calls in with an issue. The tech needs to send the ticket to a currently unavailable escalation.
    a. Inform the user of your next action and state the following, "Someone will reach out within (x timeframe)."
    b. Notate the ticket with that communication.
    c. Before hanging up, ask them, "Is there anything else I can assist with?"
2. You are updating something, and it will cause an outage.
    a. Send a communication to the business of what will be down, why you are bringing it down, and the expected time to return to service.
    b. Explain the benefits of the update to the team and provide a communication lane for any questions.
3. You have completed their work and reached out to verify.
    a. Explain that the issue is fixed and you want permission to close the ticket.
    b. Have an agreed-upon timeframe with the business in which your IT team can close the ticket if the user does not reply within a certain length of time.

Once the organization sees that the IT department is serious and accurate with its communications, it will build trust in what it says it will do. Over-communication is critical, especially at first. Also, remember this, no matter how excellent your communication plan is, there will be users who ignore every communication and will be caught "blindsided" by the change or outage. If the IT team has communicated thoroughly enough, these "blindsided" employees' leaders will handle these issues for the IT team.

The IT Department needs to set expectations on when and how to contact IT with the business, and IT leadership needs to hold the line on those expectations. **The on-call phone is for issues that absolutely cannot wait until business hours.** In the above story, Rita needed her email "right now!" In reality, her request likely could have waited until the morning. Corporate America has adopted the idea of a 24-hour workday. However, we are stating that work-life balance is paramount, and the cost of having non-essential after-hours support is IT waste.

Mental Health America Offers the following (Index 3 #7):

> "In our rush to "get it all done" at the office and at home, it's easy to forget that as our stress levels spike, our productivity plummets. Stress can zap our concentration, make us irritable or depressed, and harm our personal and professional relationships."

Changing the corporate mentality of "get it all done now" is not easy. We are focusing on the IT Help Desk since the IT team gets the brunt of after-hour work requests. IT leadership needs to work with the organization to develop and set clear guidelines on what an emergency worthy of after-hours support looks like.

Tech Republic offers a brief outline of "IT Emergencies" (Index 4 #8):

- **When the problem affects more than one person**. If an entire team, department, or building is cut off from e-mail or other network services, that's an emergency.
- **When the problem affects money**. People get ugly when you mess with their food or their money. If the payroll department calls and says they can't do the check run, that's an emergency.

- **When the problem affects a vice president.** At first blush, you might think that tech support employees rush to help a vice president or other company executives purely for political reasons, but that's not always true. If a vice president can't receive or send e-mail, it prevents the executive from managing the people and processes that get products out the door and money in the bank. Tech support requests from company honchos are definitely emergencies.

It's not an emergency when…

If an end user's machine goes down, it may or may not constitute an emergency. While waiting for tech support to be available, that individual may be able to log on to the network and use a spare laptop or a shared machine.

There's also no emergency simply because a user can't find a file, can't get an application to run, or needs help installing or using a piece of software. Is it a tech support emergency if the printer runs out of paper? Absolutely not, in most cases. In many organizations, the users are expected to replace printer paper (see the chapter, "The Hell of an Uneducated Employee"). There simply aren't that many occasions when a single user absolutely, positively has to print something. It is an emergency when an entire department cannot print, especially the warehouse and delivery operations.

Your organization must have clear guidelines for when an employee should call the after-hours on-call phone. IT leadership must be the goalkeeper on this boundary (see the chapter, "The Hell of Leadership"). The on-call IT employee must be able to make a good judgment call on what can and cannot wait until business hours. The non-IT staff must also be held accountable for making too many or too extreme of a request. A salesperson calling the on-call desk ten times in an evening for an issue that can wait until the next day is a form of bullying and should not be tolerated. Non-IT individuals communicating with the IT staff should carry the same respect as all other communication in the organization.

The IT team must also honor the on-call system and treat the calls that come in and are worthy of an emergency. The on-call IT agent should be as professional and attentive as during business hours.

Below is our IT On-call Guide:

1. If possible, staff at least six (6) agents, so an agent is never on call more than every six weeks. Never have less than four (4) available (see the chapter, "The Hell of Hiring, Firing, and Training").
2. When an agent is on call, they should be able to work from home that week or leave an hour early each day.
    a. This ensures they can take calls as soon as the on-call phone goes active.
3. The on-call week is Tuesday through Monday.
    a. This allows the on-call agent to close and continue weekend issues on Monday, and if needed, debrief for the next hand-off.
4. The week after on-call will typically include a Friday off for a three-day weekend.
    a. Even if no calls come in, the agent must be compensated for their lack of weekend freedom.
    b. Let your agent flex the day to anytime that same week.
5. The agent is permitted 15 minutes to respond to a call.
    a. Implement a routinized system users can contact to handle the escalations (read more in the chapter, "The Hell of IT Expenditure").
        i. After 3 missed calls (~45 minutes), the system calls the IT Manager.
        ii. After 3 missed calls to the manager, the IT Manager's leader is called.
        iii. The reporting end user should only call once. The on-call system should handle the repeat calls.

IT support is ultimately human support, supported by humans for humans. Having agreed-upon boundaries, needs, and fulfillment criteria are crucial for all healthy relationships. This is no difference in the relationship between your IT Department and the organization.

Hell Desk To Help Desk

Expectations go beyond users. The IT Help Desk agents must have firm guidelines on what is expected of them in their job performance. These must be solid metrics defined by the IT leadership. The IT leader must dig in and find that singular metric to champion their team (see the chapter, "The Hell of IT Leadership"). The IT leader must actively recruit and reward agents who excel at these metrics.

One expectation is often overlooked: the expectation that IT teams can function with minimal staffing and non-competitive salaries. This takes us to our next hell!

The Hell of Hiring, Training, and Firing

It is your first day as an IT Help Desk Agent. You have been the go-to person for your friends and family for IT help your entire life. You have built your own computer, set up a reliable home network, and can easily navigate any issue you have come across thus far. You have just graduated from a two-year college with an associate's degree in computer science. You are excited about starting to work at this company, and it has long been a dream of yours to turn your joy of computers into a paid profession.

You arrive early for your first day of work. You purchased a collection of ties and spent over an hour last night trying to decide which one to wear. You are happy with the simple baby blue one as it compliments your shirt.

The receptionist shows you to the IT room; it is dark, messy, and empty. All of the desks look claimed, so you grab a chair in the back of the room and wait.

At 8:30, someone else finally wanders in.

"Oh," they say, "who are you?"

You introduce yourself and explain that it is your first day as a Help Desk agent.

"Well," says the other person who still has not introduced themselves, "just wait here until the manager gets here."

Hell Desk To Help Desk

You sit back down and repeat this greeting to two more employees who show up, and you continue to introduce yourself to others over the next few hours. Still no sign of the manager.

You eventually see that the desk by the door is not taken and ask, "Is that anyone's desk?"

"That's the on-call desk," replies the bald one, "so when you're on call, you sit there."

"Is there a desk for me?" you ask.

"Ask the manager," he replies.

"Where is the manager?"

"Who knows? We can go weeks without seeing him."

You spend the next three days sitting in the same chair not completing any work or doing much of anything. You know there should be paperwork and training and much more that must be completed before day one. None of the three other employees seem interested in helping. You observe for a few days and realize that this job is not what you thought it would be. You envisioned assisting people with their computers, much like how you helped your friends and family. The three people you have met seem mostly interested in goofing off and eating.

Finally, on Thursday, the manager makes an appearance.

"Well, hello," says the manager, who also mispronounces your name, "nice tie."

You ask about your desk and any paperwork that you need to complete.

"A desk, a desk," he scratches his head, "you can have the one by the door."

The bald tech protests, "This is the on-call desk."

"Well, this new guy can go on call right away," replies the manager. "Now, for paperwork, head to HR on the third floor and ask what you need to do and when you need to do it by. I have no idea."

You spend the rest of the day and most of Friday in HR filling out government forms and documents.

It is not until your second week that you finally get to start learning about your new job. There is no structured training, just a 'here is your computer, phone, and company email.'

You ask about how you get and track work, and they reply by saying, 'here is your phone, here is your computer, here is your email.'

After a few days of digging and struggling, you come to a realization. There are over three hundred pieces of work that need to be attended to. *How did they get so far behind? Why is there no onboarding? Why is there no training? What happened to the last agent?*

Welcome to "The Hell of Hiring, Training, and Firing." This is the hell that is most ignored and least discussed. The IT department faces challenges at all three phases of an IT employee's life cycle: hiring, training, and firing. The hiring process for most IT teams is to review hundreds of two-page resumes, interview a dozen candidates for up to an hour each, talk about the candidates in one meeting, and then pick the best one. This limited exposure and outdated recruiting method is often a cause of many future IT headaches and hells. Complicating this is the fact that most corporations have lengthy procedures to fire an employee, but very simple hiring procedures. To further add to the complications, most organizations do not have a training budget for their IT staff and employees (see the chapter, "The Hell of an Uneducated Employee").

For most organizations, the training for IT employees is non-existent. They rely on certifications, experience, and the simple idea that they should 'know how to do their job.' There are more complexities to handling the IT of an organization's Help Desk than just 'fixing computers.' Even if you do find the most highly experienced and knowledgeable tech in all of creation, they will still need to learn the unique nuances of the organization's IT systems.

I can guarantee that your organization's employee exit procedures (at least, involuntary ones) go like this: You decided to terminate an employee, so the frantic manager calls and says, 'remove their access.' The IT team has no procedures and thus rush to remember all the systems and ways the employee may have access. It's a mess, and some system is always forgotten… often the corporate chat system.

So, how do we fix these three things? Let's start with hiring.

You cannot correctly judge a person by a resume and one-hour interview. Too often, we have seen phenomenal interviews turn into poor employees. We have also seen poor interviews turn into fantastic employees. How can we improve the recruiting, interviewing, and hiring processes?

The first piece of advice that we recommend is to use a contract vendor and have all new employees on a prolonged interview for six months. Have a clear understanding with the vendor that you will exercise your right to fire on demand if the employee does not fill all of your expectations. Work with multiple vendors and let them know you are using multiple vendors. Contract vendors have extensive recruiting networks and pools of potential candidates ready to go on-demand. A strong IT leader will build a relationship with the vendors and communicate a clear understanding of expectations from candidates (see more in the chapter, "The Hell of Leadership"). Provide a screening skills, customer service, and problem-solving test for the contract vendors to pre-test and screen employees before you even interview.

When recruiting, you are looking for three specific skills:

1. Customer Service
2. Problem-solving
3. IT knowledge and skills

The most critical feature of a Help Desk skill is customer service. This is not true for many other IT teams but is paramount for the end-user facing

Help Desk. Your agents will interact with users dozens of times throughout the day and must possess the invaluable skill of communicating with others. Poor customer service will affect employee perception of the IT department and corrode the culture of the IT team (see how hard these are to correct in the chapters, "The Hell of Perception" and "The Hell of Culture"). An agent with strong customer service skills will create a positive experience when interacting with users. **These customer service-focused agents know how to use voice inflection and probing questions to partner with users and make interactions positive *and* enjoyable.** Users will be far more patient with an agent who appears caring and invested in solving their issue.

When looking for this customer service skill set during the recruiting process, there are a few key things to note:

1. A prior position in a customer service role, ideally in retail, restaurant, and hospitality, or call centers.
2. Do they keep eye contact, speak clearly, and ask relevant questions during the interview?
3. Do they email the interviewers a pre-interview introduction and post-interview thank you?

During the interview process, it is ideal to first have a phone interview to get a sense of the potential agent's phone demeanor. During the phone interview, roleplay some troubleshooting scenarios and see how you feel about the interactions. Many individuals have poor face-to-face skills but possess excellent over the phone skills. The opposite is also true - we have seen phenomenal face-to-face interacting agents flounder when on the phone and helping remotely.

During the in-person interview, look for the universally understood 'classical tells.' Are they appropriately dressed for the interview? Are they timely and prepared? Do they ask thoughtful questions? Do they engage in the interview, or are they passive and shy? **A potential agent who has experience dealing with the interpersonal stress of customers will be able to manage the interview stress and appear calm and in control during interviews.**

The second most important skill to look for in potential candidates is problem-solving. This is the hardest of the three to find in pre-testing and

Hell Desk To Help Desk

interviews. Simple questions that have no singular answer allow you to feel how agents will approach issues they do not necessarily know how to fix.

Some sample questions we have used:

1. Walk me through how to make an omelet.
2. What college course would you teach, and why?
3. You get home, and there are thousands of mosquitoes; what do you do?

There is no one correct answer to any of these questions as the questions themselves are seemingly unimportant. What these do is create a situation with no clear direction so you can evaluate their answer and their thought process of how they get there. Do they approach the problems with curiosity and desire to provide solutions, or are they hesitant and afraid to proceed? Do they enjoy the challenge of the questions or struggle to respond? The way they handle your curveball of a question will reflect how they will react when working with employees and presented with a situation they do not know the answer to. We also want interviewees to ask questions and explore possible options to answer these successfully. If they just respond and do not ask for clarification, this often signals their inability to seek better answers and help when struggling. If they are floundering during these questions, they will react similarly when working with an end-user, and the user will sense their doubt and hesitancy. A skilled agent will sound and act confident, even if they do not always know what to do. This confidence comes from having solved complex issues in the past. **Agents confident in their ability to find solutions will display this confidence on calls with end-users, ultimately building their clients' confidence in their skills and ability to find a feasible solution.**

The last skill we are looking for is also the least important, but companies far too often put the highest emphasis on this skill: technical abilities. If your organization has a well-documented knowledge base containing the standard troubleshooting steps for most IT issues, technical skills become secondary to the other three (see the chapter, "The Hell of IT Expenditure). **In reality, anyone can be taught how to troubleshoot basic computer issues.** Customer service and problem-solving are far harder to teach and are often personality-based. To be clear, we are not saying to hire someone with no previous IT experience. Still, we must understand that Help Desk opportunities are considered entry-level positions that lean more on customer service and problem-solving skills than IT skills. If they are truly strong in the first two skills, they will quickly learn the third and become an asset to your team.

What you should avoid when choosing applicants for an entry-level Help Desk interview/position:

- An applicant with many years of Help Desk experience.
- An applicant who states they are a 'gamer.'
- An applicant who writes with grammar and typographic errors.

An applicant with many years of Help Desk experience. You may be asking yourself, *but isn't experience good?* Yes, it is, to an extent. If a tech has never exceeded the entry-level Help Desk and has twenty years of experience, they have likely reached their peak. You want candidates that will improve and grow, not those that are content and comfortable. Promoting Help Desk to advanced teams improves the overall IT department. These "level 1 career techs" have no training outside of work. They have proven they have no desire to grow and learn skills beyond the basics. Every leader we interviewed said the same: avoid lifetime Help Desk agents.

An applicant who states they are a 'gamer.' The vast majority of IT help desk agents are gamers. But, if they're basing their entire ability to troubleshoot and help end-users with their passion for gaming, they have missed the objective of being a Help Desk team member. Too often, leaders see "gamers" come in, and all they really know how to do is turn on the computer and install pirated software illegally. True professionals will focus more on their skills and experience than their love and interest.

Grammar and typographic errors. It hopefully raises a red flag when you read resumes that have misspellings and incorrect punctuation. If candidates aren't taking the time to edit and meticulously review their resume correctly, you can expect them to perform similarly in their day-to-day work. These typically lazy individuals are self-centered and entitled, regularly expecting the world to be handed to them.

Hell Desk To Help Desk

A note on salary: Pay your employees enough to where money is not a consideration if they accept a job, but not so much that they are just chasing an impressive paycheck. If your candidate pool is lacking, your salary may be too low for the market. If applying candidates are overqualified, you are offering too much.

Keep in mind that you do want to hire individuals who will eventually get promoted, so ask yourself why this former server administrator (or other high-level IT position) is seeking an entry-level position. It may be, however, that they want to get their foot in the door if your organization has a strong reputation; if this is the case, then they may be a safe hire. It may also be that this applicant failed at server administration and is looking to step down and reevaluate their career path… another possibly safe hire since it is not uncommon to re-path yourself in IT. It is additionally possible that they want an 'easy' or 'stress-free' position. Avoid these slackers who are avoiding hard work, commonly known as a "Not My Job Nick."

Have a trusted committee of individuals you bring in to help with the interviews and the hiring decisions. Involve non-IT individuals from around the organization to also be a part of this committee; the perspective and insight from a non-IT point of view can be very valuable.

For hiring decisions, make the offer to the contract vendor and work with them for the onboarding process. If you read the previous chapters and already have an excellent KB (knowledge base) system, you know that you should have a well-documented training and orientation schedule during the onboarding.

Congratulations on hiring a new employee! Now, what do you do with them? If you followed our advice in the chapter, "The Hell of IT Expenditure," then you have purchased a centralized storage system for all IT resources, materials, paperwork, and company unique knowledge. This will create a much easier employee onboarding process as they will be able to reference the KB system during their early days and not have to be as much of a burden on the existing employees. Provide the new employee with step-by-step instructions on what needs to be done, where they do it, and the deadline for completion.

The first few weeks of an employee's time with an organization should fulfill these milestones:

- By day three, all HR activities must be complete.
- By day five, all employee introductions must be completed.
- By the end of week three, all training must be completed.
- When the employee reaches their one-month anniversary, they should be able to work independently on basic and common issues without assistance.

If an employee cannot meet these milestones and it is your first time using this system, go back and evaluate your training. If you have had employees go through the training and meet the one-month milestone in the past, fire this new employee. Ask the contract vendor to send you another candidate and move on. **The most significant advantage of using a vendor is that you can quickly fire *and* hire candidates.** Many organizations have a prolonged termination process, but using a vendor for hiring will bypass this.

When you improve and expand upon your in-house training, it must include videos and peer shadowing. Too often, we see either no training or the training only including some basic PowerPoints. Have your experienced agents record "how-to" videos of all basic tasks that must be done. Work with your advanced agents and have this library of accessible videos constantly growing and updated. Incorporate these videos into self-paced presentations and provide post-instruction evaluations to ensure they have retained the information. Create a final exam and if you notice a weakness in any areas, have them repeat the training they failed. If your video and training library is sufficient, most training can and should be self-paced. **Offering self-paced training gives you insight into the trainee's abilities, drive, and dedication.** After completing the formal training, utilize a feedback form to continually improve upon your instructional system.

Employee onboarding and training should go as such:

1. Week 1: HR paperwork and employee introductions (how to log time and log into the systems needed to complete work, i.e. email, knowledge base, ticketing, and chat systems).

2. Week 2: Formal training on what and who you support.
3. Week 3: Shadowing of a current employee.
4. Week 4: A current employee watches the new hire and coaches.
5. Week 5: Employee should be mostly self-sufficient.

Do not rush the training; give your new employee a chance to adjust to the role and be successful. Weeks three and four are crucial, as they will allow for the mentor/mentee relationship to develop among your employees. We want your new employees to view colleagues as a viable resource. **Leading training and being a mentor improves your existing employees' overall impression of the new hire within the organization.**

Once an employee is onboarded, **do not stop mentoring them**. This is also, and especially true for all existing employees. Have your IT leader research and develop courses that will benefit and fill the gaps on your team. Non-IT courses on customer service, public speaking, and problem-solving are all beneficial for your entire team. Assign your colleagues books to read (like this one!) and enable discussions about what was read. These "soft skill" courses will improve your team's ability to interact with users and work towards improving the perception of the team to the greater organization (see the chapter, "The Hell of Impressions"). Send your team to IT and Help Desk conferences and pay for advanced training. If you balk at this expense, go back and read "The Hell of IT Expenditure." You must have missed something important. Having a highly trained team reduces downtime for the company as the more skilled team can quickly address the issues.

Have your team host training for the entire organization. Having the IT team train others will help improve the skillsets of the team and the employees they assist while also enhancing the perception of the organization as well. Be sure to read the chapters, "The Hell of an Uneducated Employee" and "The Hell of Impressions," on how these sessions have infinite value.

A secondary benefit of training your team is that they begin to feel their worth for the corporation. When you invest in their development, they feel valued and feel that the corporation is vested in their success. **When you send your IT team to conferences or training, they view this as a perk or a reward.** These are fun experiences that refresh their love for IT support.

The final phase of the employee life cycle is exiting. There are three ways your employees may leave your team:

1. Involuntary
2. Voluntary
3. Natural

The **involuntary exit** is pretty self-explanatory: the organization has chosen to fire an employee for some reason. If you have followed our advice, your IT agents are under their six-month initial contract, and this is as easy as calling the vendor, telling them you no longer want this employee, and to send another. We have seen that employees who make it to six months without issues will usually make their whole career without problems. Your organization will have its own procedures and protocols for employee termination. All termination processes have one thing in common, however- the day finally comes when the employee exits the organization.

Your organization must have the IT team ready to go before you terminate an employee. Their access must be removed before they know what is happening to avoid sabotage or retaliation. In 1996, newly-fired Omega Engineering Corp. employee Timothy Lloyd set up a digital bomb that deleted all of the company's programs and cost them $10 million in sales and contracts. It is one of many horror stories about resentful IT employees that wreak havoc on company computer systems as retaliation. A Symantec study in 2013 showed that half of the employees who left or lost their jobs that year kept confidential corporate data, with 40% planning to use it in their new job! Don't set yourself up to have a "Timothy Lloyd revenge" on your company!

Your Help Desk team is involved in all employee termination, IT, and non-IT employees. Your team must be trained and drilled in the steps of removing all IT access. If you read and followed the chapter's ideas, "The Hell of IT Expenditure," you have a KB system. In this overarching system, there must be a detailed document on every system and how to remove access to it. Have your IT team practice running through employee exits. Their goal is to have a terminated employee 100% out of every system in fifteen minutes. Your IT leader will have to plan and practice these drills. The IT leader will work with

HR and organization leaders on the best way to communicate when a termination is needed. The organization's leaders also need to realize they are equally susceptible to being terminated, requiring accountability and protection for the organization to prevent retaliation and sabotage. **While most employees will exit quietly and with dignity, the possibility for destructive and inappropriate exists and must be accounted for.**

The second way an employee leaves is through a **voluntary exit.** This could happen in one of two ways: They may be leaving the company entirely, or they may be promoted/transferred to another team within the organization. If they are leaving the company altogether, treat their exit (as far as IT access goes) the same as a firing. Many organizations will choose to release an employee the day they give notice. Whenever the company organization decides that it is an employee's last day, run through the same steps as a firing.

If the employee is internally transferring or being promoted, these will merit access changes. While some accesses will be removed, their access to the standard systems (email, chat, etc.) will likely remain untouched. **Your IT leader must work with every team and get a complete list of all the access needed for employees of the specific team**. Keep this list in your KB system, and if your team is capable, automate the changes.

The third type of exit is a **natural exit**. This is when the employee leaves the workforce entirely: Death or retirement. Even though this exit is very low risk, treat it the same as a termination. On their last day, remove their access using the same process for termination.

These employee life cycles also apply to the IT leader. They must be the standard for which all other IT employees follow. The way you handle your employees throughout their employment is a direct reflection of the IT team's culture.

This leads us to our next hell...

The Hell of Culture

This is it, the day you have worked so hard for your entire life. You are finally managing an IT team! You have been working your way through the various IT fields, gaining experience, reading books (such as this one!), and training with mentors. You have your MBA from an accredited university. Finally, the day you dreamed, worked, studied, and sacrificed for has arrived. The interview was remote, and you have never seen your office or even met the team.

You arrive an hour early with breakfast for your new team, bagels and coffee. The building is modern and clean, with metal framing and sparkling glass windows. The shiny floors glimmer, and your shoes give a comfortable squeak as you walk. The ultra-modern lobby is impressive in its magnitude and cleanliness. The receptionist greets you warmly and walks you back to the IT Room. As you walk the immaculate halls of this new building, you daydream of the incredible office that awaits you.

Then reality hits.

You reach the end of a hallway that appears darker than the rest (it must be your imagination). The modern glass walls have given way to cold concrete blocks with peeling paint. *Is this the same building?* You reach a door with the word "Technology" on a placard. Somehow, the IT department has the only wooden door in the whole building. The receptionist fumbles for a key. Where every other door had modern electronic locks with RFID sensors, the IT department used a traditional metal key. She unlocks the door and steps back.

"Here is your new home," says the receptionist with a smile as she scurries away.

Hell Desk To Help Desk

You peek in and survey the room. It is dark; a few blue, green, and red lights twinkle through the darkness. There are sounds of fans running, some sounding like they are on their last leg. You can smell old food, spilled drinks, and what you think is body odor. *Yikes.*

You reach around the door frame and feel for a light. Instead, you touch metal and shock yourself. You pull out your phone and turn on the flashlight. You aim the flashlight along the wall at what shocked you. *A-ha.* There is an exposed wire coming out of the bottom of the switch. You use the phone to switch on the lights. The fluorescent lights blink on painfully.

The room looks cramped and screams, "go away." The carpet is dull, worn, and torn. There are six desks with privacy walls, all facing away from each other. None of the workspaces are visible from the door, so all a guest sees upon entry are the back of six desks. Each desk is messy, with laptops buried under computer parts and food wrappers. Each desk has monitors too large for the workstation, and the chairs are all stained and torn.

You walk past the gaggle of desks to the rear of the room where you think you see an existing workbench under a pile of old computers and parts. The fridge in the corner hums and clanks. You find the "IT Manager's" office door and push it open. It stops halfway, hitting a desk. You peek around and see the "way-too-large-for-this-room" desk arranged so the manager can face the door and hide his computer monitor. The whole setup reeks of unfriendliness.

You place the bagels and coffee on the refrigerator and get to work re-arranging your office.

8:00 AM hits, and you are still alone. You have practiced your welcome speech all month, and the perfect moment has passed with no one to hear it.

At 8:32, your first employee wanders in.

"Morning," you chirp.

"Who are you?" asks the skinny and bald man.

"I am the new IT Manager," you reply. "Who are you?"

"Andy," he ends the sentence bluntly.

"Hello Andy," you say, "do you work here?"

"Yes," he quickly runs to one of the desks and buries his head in the monitor.

"'Do you know where everyone is?" you call after Andy.

"Not here," he replies sharply.

At 9:05, there is a knock on the front door, and Andy doesn't even respond. You peer around the desk to see if he is awake. He is clicking away at some screen. You walk to the door and open it.

"Oh, are you waiting for help?" asks the well-dressed young woman.

"No, I am the new IT Manager," you reply.

"Oh, good luck,'" she replies and turns away down the hall.

At 9:30, another person walks in.

"Hello," you say to the new face.

"Who are you?" asks the heavy-set man.

"I am the new IT Manager," you reply. "Who are you?"

He gives you a disapproving look, "Nick."

"Pleased to meet you, Nick," you say as you offer a handshake.

He ignores your hand, turns to his desk, and sits down. You consider chastising him for being here at 9:30 but decided… *not on the first day.*

Hell Desk To Help Desk

At 10:07, your third and final employee walks in.

"Hello," you say to the new face.

"Who are you?" asks the obese man.

"I am the new IT Manager," you reply. "Who are you?"

"Steve," he replies through a burp. He wipes his hand on his pants and offers a handshake.

"Did not know you were starting today," says Steve.

You return the shake. Steve drops your hand, scurries back to the refrigerator, and chugs an energy drink. You try to find a place to speak to all three employees, but there is no such area. *How is there no designated meeting area?* You stand by the workbench and call your new crew to the back to introduce yourself.

"Gentlemen," you call across the room, "can you join me back here?"

"Why?" calls Nick immediately.

"I want to introduce myself," you say, "Can you three join me back here?"

"We can hear you from here," "says Nick.

"Gentlemen," you plead, "please, I want to look at each of you while I talk."

"No need," says Andy.

"I want to make this team great," you say.

"So did the last guy," replies Nick, "and now he has that sweet job at that firm on the beach."

"This is my dream," you say, starting your speech, "to lead an IT team in support of a business."

Nick stands up, "Look, man, no one wants to work in IT. We just end up here until we can sell an app or, like the last manager, get an easy job working for a law firm."

"I love supporting people," you reply, "don't you get joy from seeing the users smile?"

All three laugh hard.

"You new to IT?" asks Nick.

Steve chimes in, "yeah, I remember my early days, back when I liked this job."

"You three don't like helping users?" you ask.

"No," says Nick, "just here for the paycheck."

Not the best first day. Much of this rings true: sloppy office, tardy techs, bad attitudes, and no joy or sense of wonder in the job. What causes this? Why do so many IT departments resemble and act like this? Welcome to "The Hell of Culture."

It is far too common that the IT department is a borderline frat house… something more akin to an 80s sex romp than a high-tech adventure story. How do we fix this? How do we make our IT team a pleasure to interact with? How do we make our team excited about assisting the end-user? How do we encourage our team to aggressively look for improvement and seek out and destroy the current IT problems within an organization?

Here are the 5 conditions that drag down IT culture (and their chapters for review):

1. Non-existent IT expenditure ("The Hell of IT Expenditure")

2. Poorly educated corporate staff ("The Hell of an Uneducated Employee")
3. Incompetent staffing ("The Hell of Hiring, Training, and Firing")
4. Low corporate expectations ("The Hell of Expectations")
5. Ineffective leadership ("The Hell of Leadership")

You should notice how each of the above is one of our IT Hells. IT Hells produce a hostile culture. These are ranked 1 to 5, with 1 being a minor cause of poor culture and 5 being a major cause. We delve more into how each of these creates their own hell in their chapters and how to address the issues and their demons. We will spend this chapter discussing how these hells ruin the culture of an IT department and inadvertently create the worst hell of them all: **The Hell of Culture.** This chapter highlights our second to last hell, which is often the combination of the other hells as they grow to fester each other.

Our first culture-killing Hell is a mismanaged IT budget. Under (and over) spending can affect your IT team and their performance. An IT team can become discouraged if they cannot purchase the equipment needed to perform their jobs successfully. Conversely, an IT team can become complacent and rely too heavily on expenditure for fancy gadgets to solve their problems, potentially hindering their creativity and problem-solving skills. We must not allow the IT team to spoil themselves with costly IT equipment. Walking around the office with new $7,000 gaming laptops while the "rank and file" squeak by with three-year old-laptops will undoubtedly taint the IT image among other staff.

On the contrary, having mediocre equipment can give an organization the impression that the IT department is mismanaging the budget. Poor IT funding allocation creates a sense of waste and a haphazardly managed IT department. This climate will quickly creep into the actions and behaviors of the IT crew and the organization staff at large. If the IT leadership cannot manage its own purse strings, how can it possibly manage the operations of the whole department? IT leadership must be good stewards of the IT budget and hold the team accountable for proper spending. More on this concept to come in the chapter, "The Hell of Leadership."

Our second culture-killing Hell is a poorly educated corporate staff. The IT department must be a source of education, skill, and know-how. By being the go-to for all corporate IT-related training, the IT department will be viewed more as an ally than a foe. As we discussed in the chapter, "The Hell of an Uneducated Employee," **if the IT department can heighten the general "tech-savvy" of an organization, it will, in turn, be more understanding of IT needs.** This understanding will elevate the overall IT culture of an organization.

An IT team that partners with and simultaneously educates the organization will create positive relationships. These relationships build a bond between the IT department and the organization. These bonds will foster more than just a positive perception of the IT department, genuine awe and curiosity as these "technical wizards" keep the lights on day after day. This education also helps prevent the fourth hell, "The Hell of Expectations."

But first, we must venture to the third culture-killing hell: incompetent IT staffing. This hell is placed above the previous two because without a sound and skilled IT staff, there is no escape from the two lesser hells. If the IT staff is untrained and uninformed on properly evaluating, proposing, budgeting, and ultimately purchasing IT needs, they will give way to "The Hell of IT Expenditure." If an IT staff member does not have the heart of an educator, nor even the desire to take the time and interact with the staff lovingly and encouragingly, they will not be able to prevent or escape "The Hell of an Uneducated Employee."

Beyond simply hiring competent, caring, and driven employees, the IT department must also be dedicated to training and developing them. A staff that sees the organization investing in their advancements will feel valued, and in return, offer value to the corporation. This feeling of value will encourage employees to perform in ways that build and promote the IT culture. The same could be said for the organization as a whole. **If the organization experiences the IT team growing and training others, this will change the perception of the team.** They can transform from the idea of being "just another lazy team" to a partner team that is vested in the success of the greater organization.

The fourth culture-killer is low corporate expectations. This hell takes the longest to improve the culture out of. Once an organization views the IT department negatively, it can take years to recover. Word of mouth is the most effective advertisement, and if the members of the organization think the IT department is awful, they will share their thoughts with anyone they can. Word of mouth and its reach has been amplified with the rise of the social media era. The last thing you want is a corporate executive badmouthing the IT team on their Twitter account.

This culture hell is combated best through education, training, and meaningful interactions. As discussed in the chapter, "The Hell of an Uneducated Employee," an educated employee can become a culture champion. **A stupid employee is always dangerous.** It is critical that the IT department arrange a time to host training sessions for your organization. These sessions will serve to educate the organization's employees on the IT department & equipment and how to solve problems within the IT realm. The hidden benefit of these meetings is that the organization and the IT department get to spend time in a positive and nurturing environment, further improving the perception and culture of the IT team.

The last culture-killer is "The Hell of Leadership." This hell is the most corrosive but is frequently the easiest to fix. An IT leader who allows the hells to grow and fester is the worst of the IT Demons. This leader will allow other demons to flourish and multiply. One easy way to deal with this? Fire the incompetent IT leader. This is a harsh and direct action. The longer road, however, is to hold the leader accountable for their actions and set clear guidelines and expectations on what is acceptable moving forward. **This leader must lead from a culture perspective first.** Their focus needs to be improving corporate perceptions and enamoring the organization with the work of the IT team.

There are many ways to encourage a positive culture from a "grassroots" level. **Humans love being part of a team.** We see this in all aspects of our life. People root for their favorite sports team, champion their favorite movie series (Star Wars or Star Trek), argue Marvel vs. DC, and bicker about the better video gaming system, Xbox vs .PlayStation. There's a tribalism and a competitiveness that exists in all of us. We need to take advantage of this innate drive with our team. When we do, the results are incredible. We have seen tremendous support for each other when teams are formed and clearly identified.

Employees identify each other as part of a team and support and encourage each other with proper branding. The place we see it start with the highest success is with uniforms, where a group shares a common image and common theme that they can foster in each other. **The simplest thing you can do for your team to encourage team building is to purchase polo shirts with your team logo.** It could be a shirt with your company's name on the chest, and it could say 'IT Support' on the sleeve, for example. We recommend ordering various styles, like long sleeve shirts, sweaters, and t-shirts. Have the team involved in the design and then provide them for free. If you want your team to wear these uniforms and ultimately elevate the dress code (see the chapter, "The Hell of Impressions"), it's vital that you do not charge the employee. You can't tell employees to wear a specific shirt and not provide the shirts. Doing so will negatively affect morale and work against your original goal of building a robust IT culture. It will not be seen as a team-building effort, but as enforcement for no real reason.

You could also provide employees with other company-branded items like water bottles, mousepads, phone cases, and stickers- fun little tchotchkes that they can use/display to let others know they are part of a team. As we mentioned earlier, humans love to be a part of something, a member of a team, a part of a tribe. Having these branded items that your work provides, or at least at the bare minimum, makes available for purchase, goes a long way into fostering this team feeling and culture. Branded items also contribute to the IT team's recognition and professionalism throughout the organization.

Once your team looks like a team, start treating them like one. The IT leader's primary job is to encourage and motivate the team. They must be coaches and leaders, not bosses (see the chapter, "The Hell of Leadership"). When looking for ways to quickly build team culture, relationships, and motivation, we found a simple solution: **The single most excellent motivator across the board is free food.** The simple act of buying lunch for your team, for example, yields tremendous results towards motivation. Make buying food a common and established reward for operational achievements. Host lunch events that coincide with holidays. You can have a 4th of July BBQ, a Thanksgiving potluck, or even a summer 'salad bar.' Get the team involved in planning to encourage involvement, community, and bonding. One leader we interviewed once brought in a hot plate and made pancakes, eggs, and bacon for their team for breakfast.

Hell Desk To Help Desk

The team really responded to the leader making them breakfast in a personable, relatable, fun way. Be that as it may, we do advise against providing meals too frequently. We have seen teams in these cases start to expect the food, and when food is not provided, they feel like they have lost a benefit. When employees feel slighted, they begin to foster a negative working culture.

Using the reward and recognition program we advised you to purchase in "The Hell of IT Expenditure," recognizing Help Desk agents who perform above and beyond will cultivate pride, positivity, and motivation. When an agent has earned enough points for a major reward (TV, cruise, etc.), celebrate the exciting achievement with the whole team. Host a ceremony or party to present the earned reward to the deserving agent. This lets the other agents know that these larger rewards are achievable. This celebration also motivates others to strive to earn these prizes. Employees like gifts, but they also like and want to be recognized before their team.

The last culture-building effort we have seen have great success: out-of-work team activities. We recommend having a non-work-related event for your IT team at least once a quarter. Be intentional when choosing an activity for your team. Here are some ideas to get you started:

1. Buy out a movie screening.
2. An airsoft/paintball outing.
3. An end-of-year formal dinner.
4. Escape Room challenge.
5. Video game parties with snacks and booze (after hours).

Team building will naturally encourage the Help Desk to find common goals. This is the definition of a team: a group working for a common goal. When any team is formed, they immediately look for that goal. The leader's responsibility is to guide the team toward the correct goal. We will elaborate on finding this goal and how to hold the team accountable for it in the chapter, "The Hell of Leadership." **Once the specific and measurable metric is clearly identified, your team will begin to champion this metric and hold each other accountable.** You will have "champions" on your team who will rise up, take ownership of the metric, and push the rest of the team to achieve. Recognize and acknowledge these champions when they buy in and embrace the culture because, without a clear and straightforward goal, your team will struggle and spin their wheels as they chase a non-unified front.

A team can only identify and be aimed at the correct work with a passionate, dedicated, and competent leader.

This leads us to our deepest and most treacherous of the IT hells, "The Hell of Leadership." *Dun dun dun.*

The Hell of Leadership

You are the COO of the organization. You already have some concerns about the IT team. It is Christmas Eve, and you are trying to leave early when there is a knock at the door.

"Come in," you say begrudgingly.

The customer service manager, Rita, walks in.

"Hello Rita," you greet.

"We have lost every phone," she says in a panic, "we can't take or send calls. We are getting loads of emails from pissed-off customers."

"Have you called IT yet?" you ask.

"How the fuck am I supposed to call them?" Rita screeches.

"Oh yeah, sorry. Enough of this," you say sternly, "I will walk down there now."

You take the elevator down to the sublevel. You expect to hear the usual loud music and goofing off from the IT room as you exit the elevator, but you are surprised to find silence. You approach the room and open the sticker-covered door. More silence. The room is empty.

Hell Desk To Help Desk

"Hello," you call out, "anyone here?"

Only silence responds.

You pick up the phone on the desk by the door. No dial tone. You grab your cell phone and call the IT manager. You can hear the sound of his ringing phone coming from the back. You walk back to his cave of an office, and you hear the phone ringing through the door. You knock on the door. No answer. You try the handle, but it's locked. You pound on the door, kicking and hammering, shaking the walls around it.

"What?!" yells a voice from beyond the door. It is the IT manager, Bob.

"We have lost all phones in the building," you yell, "open the door so we can figure this out!"

"I sent everyone home," he yells back, "it's Christmas Eve! Tell everyone we can't fix anything until Monday."

Your eyes go red with anger. You step back and recall the three years of Taekwondo training. You ready your back foot, chamber your front, and aim just next to the handle. BOOM. The door explodes open as you kick, breaking the frame. The sight horrifies you. Bob is mostly blocked by his oversized monitor, but his pants are lowered, and his hand is in his lap.

"Dear God," you yell as you avert your eyes, "dress yourself and fix the phones."

"I can't," fumbling as he dresses himself. "Andy was the phone guy, and he is at a gamer convention."

"Can anyone else fix it?" you plead.

"No," says Bob, "no one else has ever touched it."

"Fine," you reply, as you grab your cell phone and look for numbers for the rest of the IT team, "you're fired."

"What?" yells back Bob, "over a phone outage?"

"No," you yell back, "for being a sick pervert. Now get out before I call the police and have you escorted out."

"Fine," Bob shouts as he clicks a few buttons on his mouse and laughs, "best of luck, chumps." He stands up and walks out.

You work your way through two numbers when your phone rings. It's the VP of sales.

"We just lost all email!" he yells.

As he is yelling, a text comes in. It's the CFO: "We have lost all sales reports."

Over the next few minutes, as calls and texts roll in, the horror of what Bob has done reveals itself. He has wiped all systems, email, file storage, CRM, ERP, and WHM. Everything is gone. *Gone.*

Remember, these are all real stories from real people. The IT manager described here was a real person. This is the sort of demon you could face in IT leadership. This is the final and deepest of the IT Hells, **The Hell of Leadership**. This hell is the lair of **Bob the Boss.** This IT demon is the IT leader who not only fosters the other hells, but his actions actively encourage them. He will acquiesce to the demands of the lesser demons and let their whines and wails drive his decisions. Bob is driven by laziness, a desire for fame, and the sole idea of being called a "boss." Bobs are usually looking for that next promotion or freebies from vendors. Their time is spent more on self-interest than on improving the IT team.

The role of the IT leader is the most critical piece of any IT team. We have seen fabulous teams destroyed by poor leadership, just as we have seen terrible teams perform miracles under solid, focused, driven, and well-planned leadership. This chapter is focused on building that perfect, role-model IT leader.

Hell Desk To Help Desk

We will lay out exactly what the leader should be doing and focusing on and how they should be interacting with the team. This picture we are painting is for a Help Desk manager. Many of these traits and ideas will translate to other IT teams, while some will not.

First and foremost, the team must know that the leader is always aware of agent tasks and overall productivity. The IT manager must use monitoring tools (see "The Hell of IT Expenditure") to always know how much incoming work the Help Desk has, how quickly they are completing it, and how efficient each agent is. The manager will use this data for all actions and decisions. This data must be the IT manager's "Elevator Pitch."

When asked about metrics, the IT manager's reply should be along these lines: "We have about 2,000 pieces of inbound work each month, and we can close 85% at the first contact. The team averages 250 closures per agent. We have also reduced total incoming work by 12% this year." Having this knowledge readily available focuses the leader on what matters for a successful Help Desk team.

After interviewing dozens of leaders, we have simplified the guide for Help Desk leaders as follows:

The 7 Tenets of the Help Desk Leader:

1. Reduce total work.
2. Shield the team from "shoulder taps."
3. Hold the organization to the standards and expectations the IT team has established.
4. Champion and celebrate your team.
5. Be fully aware of all IT activities and productivity.
6. Be ready to get your hands dirty and help clear out any work.
7. Clearly define and simplify what the IT team should focus on.

The most paramount of all these principles is "reducing incoming work." The single most significant key to success for a Help Desk is to reduce the work. This is not an easy task. The IT leader must work with other teams and identify the issues that cause phone calls and service tickets. Being metrics-driven allows you to see the source of work, however. Once the leader has identified the "root cause" of the work source, go after the biggest first.

We interviewed one organization, and 15% of all of their end-user support calls were in one way or another related to password resets. The company had a self-service password reset portal, but users simply did not use it. The IT leader worked with the organization's leadership and started an educational campaign to ensure all users knew not about the existence and uses of the portal. During this campaign, the leader found out that some workers did not have computers and only used their passwords to log into the warehouse equipment. The leader presented data to the warehouse leadership that showed the number of hours their employees spent on the phone resetting passwords each month. Based on this data, in conjunction with the IT department, the warehouse leadership set up workstations for the sole purpose of resetting passwords throughout the warehouse. This ended up saving 15 minutes per month per employee. Fifteen minutes may not sound like much, but if this organization had 10,000 employees across all warehouses, this is a productivity savings of 2,500 hours per month across the organization.

The IT leader needs to not only look at the "big wins" but also at the minutes saved.

Sometimes the work is hidden. One organization told us a story about software access requests. The requester and the fulfilling agent would send emails back and forth, then forwarded, then replied and forwarded again, ensuring that all proper approvals were met. At first, they ignored it since no one complained. Once the IT leader dug in, he found that the agents would spend around five minutes per email. So, not a big deal yet. The leader continued to dig and found that it averaged four emails per request, so twenty minutes. Again, not a massive chunk of time. The leader kept digging and found that the number of requests was 2.500 a year. That is over 800 hours a year just spent on emails. The IT leader worked with their automation team and created an "approval process" that did not require emails, only simple yes/no buttons.

The best IT leaders know the daily processes their team works through and are continuously looking for ways to improve upon them and reduce their work.

Hell Desk To Help Desk

The "shoulder tap" is a common IT sin we often see committed. A "shoulder tap" is anytime a request for work comes into your team but it did not come in through the normal channels. Most often, it is somebody walking into the IT office or contacting a Help Desk tech directly in some form. These "shoulder taps" are often not represented in the metrics as the agent will usually just fix their issue and not create a ticket. This must be stopped at all levels. The IT leader must work with the organization to clarify that all work requests must go through the proper ticketing system (see the chapter, "The Hell of IT Expenditure"), and any urgent requests must go through the IT leader. **No one may directly contact the Help Desk agents. A capable IT leader will know precisely what his team is working on and the best choice to work on any escalations.** Hold the organization accountable for this (see "The Hell of Expectations"). This IT Leader acting as a shield of "shoulder taps" is the most overlooked but one of the most beneficial attributes of a strong IT leader. The Awkward Andys of the world will appreciate not having to speak to people as much, and the Not My Job Nicks will appreciate not having to change course suddenly. As the 'shoulder taps" and escalations come in, the IT leader can work as a filter and help decide what is truly an emergency or what simply needs a ticket. Having the leader act as the "goalkeeper" also provides a single point of contact so the IT leader can work with these upset customers directly. The Help Desk agents must be shielded from complaints and upset users. The IT leader must be the person upset users work with. As they say, this is why they are "paid the big bucks."

The IT team is often the most overlooked of all organizations, especially when doing a great job. If all is well, they are often forgotten. Usually, the only non-work request interactions the IT department receives are complaints about an outage. This is why the IT leader must celebrate and champion the team. Publish celebrations for the whole organization to acknowledge. **Buy your team lunch for no defined reason, often!** Recognize daily, weekly, monthly, and annual achievements. Use a customer/coworker feedback system that allows the agents to purchase prizes (see the chapter, "The Hell of IT Expenditure"). This recognition system must have simple prizes like gift cards and free food and top tier prizes like TVs, days off from work, cruises, etc.

The IT leader must be fully aware of their team's current and recently worked-on tasks. The IT team must also know that their leader is fully aware of its ongoings. The simplest way to do this is to post charts in the team chat of the metrics. Charts like this:

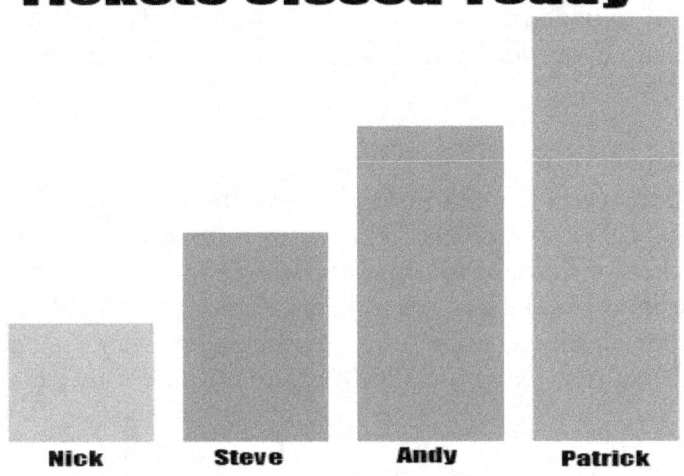

Find the metric that matters and keep it in front of your team. The above example is about tickets, but it could be calls, reviews, or anything your IT leader has found to be the metric of importance.

Post these charts regularly for your team to see. Help them recognize that you, as the IT leader, are watching and noting productivity. You will get complaints and excuses from the low performers, but **the reality is that the organization only wants results, and ticket closures are results to them.** The IT leader must be using these metrics to have meaningful conversations with the agents. Why are some completing more work? Is the graph even a fair representation of the work? Perhaps Nick is doing more complicated work, or Patrick is "cherry picking" easier work to pad and boost his stats. The IT leader should know what's going on and be able to evaluate if they are measuring the work on a one-for-one basis. In the case of this graph, it is also possible that Nick is simply slacking off, and the leader, therefore, needs to have performance conversations with this agent.

Hell Desk To Help Desk

More often than not, when an IT manager first takes over a team, there is a backlog of work. The leader must dive headfirst into the backlog and help clear it out. The IT leader is not in an "above the rest" position, nor are they the best at IT on the team. They must be honest about their abilities and be fully willing to help where they can. **Typically, the best help an IT leader can offer is reaching out to users**. Many common IT issues will self-resolve with time; reboots, updates, password resets, etc., will often resolve the most common issues.

When there is a backlog, the IT leader needs to go through the backlog and reach out to the users from these aged tickets and ask if there is still an issue. The reality is, tickets over two weeks old are usually resolved... either self-resolved or a second ticket (or third, or fourth, or fifth, etc.) was opened to fix the issue without the agent checking to see if the user already had a ticket open. We interviewed one leader who reduced the backlog by over 20% on their first week as a leader by simply asking users if they were OK and if they could close the ticket.

The IT leader must also be willing to lend an extra pair of hands for projects and time for after-hours work. Need to run cables in a building? Be there with a ladder and a smile. Need to shut down and vacuum out servers? Bring coffee and a duster. **The primary difference between a leader and a manager is that a leader can and is happily willing to do the team's work.**

As for what the team should be doing, the IT leader needs to clearly define and communicate a single metric the team should focus on. We have looked at dozens of teams and found that the goal you must push your team towards should be a very simple and "easy to measure and specify" metric. It will vary slightly from team to team based on business needs, but one of the following metrics are most common for Help Desks:

1. Tickets closed per day/month/year.
2. Agent availability to users.
3. Calls answered per day/month/year.

The organization is most satisfied with a Help Desk if they are available and able to resolve their issues on demand. Users do not want to call in and wait on the phone. The ideal experience is when they call they immediately and get a *human* who knows how to fix their issue. If you are a phone-based Help Desk with more than ten agents, have phone software able to track the agents' status (see the chapter, "The Hell of It Expenditure"). Larger teams are harder to wrangle and you will need software to help. If you are able, have your team sit in a "call center" layout with screens visibly mounted to show the metrics of calls and availability. Nothing works like peer pressure (except money and food).

Having identified the key metric, the IT leader must champion this daily and regularly. Push the team to be aware of their individual performance on that metric. Have frequent communications and discussions on the status of the metric and how this metric affects all other work. Have signs hung at the office reminding the team of the metric. Recognize the agents who are working hard at meeting the metric. This must be a core focus for the team. When agents exceed the metric, have them mentor and work with others who are not (see the chapters, "The Hell of Hiring, Training, and Firing" and "The Hell of Culture").

The leader needs to be the face of the IT Help Desk. They need to be present and active in the organization. Look for leaders who are passionate about helping users, who excel at customer service, who celebrate their team and its accomplishments, and who can communicate and be presentable (see the chapters, "The Hell of Hiring, Training, and Firing," "The Hell of Impressions," and "The Hell of Culture"). **The entire Help Desk team will follow the example set by the leader.** If the leader is aloof and uncaring, the team will be lazy and uninvolved. If the leader is present and active, the team will be motivated and engaged.

The right leader will actively work to exorcise the demons and build IT Heaven.

IT Heaven

You are the training manager for the organization. For years, you have long distrusted the IT team, but something has changed in the last few months.

You are working from home this week. It is February, and several feet of snow have closed the roads. You are cozy by the fire with a fresh cup of coffee. You work on an excel spreadsheet of your team's performance in January. You take a moment to admire your new laptop. The IT team issued what they called a "refresh" in December. You could not be happier: the laptop is quick, it turns on, connects to the VPN, and your files load right up. You had to reset your password at the end of January, but it was a simple website you had to visit, there were no issues, and it was easy to use. You begin to think back to how bad the IT team was a few years ago. You recall the nearly daily interactions you had with them as your team seemed to always have IT issues. There was no way you could have sent everyone remote with such poor IT support. You try to remember the last time you had to speak to a Help Desk agent... oh yes, it was when you onboarded a new employee. It was not even a phone call; you chatted with an agent online, and they directed you to a form to fill out, and that was it. On day one, the employee was set and ready to go.

On a whim, you decided to ask your fellow leaders if they have had any IT issues lately. You start a group chat.

You: "Hey team, I was just thinking, when was the last IT issue we had?"

Hell Desk To Help Desk

COO: "I had a team member lose access to our shared drive last week?"

You: "Did IT get it fixed?"

COO: "Yeah, on the phone and fixed in minutes. Turns out HR had accidentally changed their title, and the IT system changed their permissions accordingly."

You: "So everything worked as designed, a human error by HR broke it?"

COO: "Yup."

You: "Anyone else have a recent issue? I can't even recall the last time we called IT?"

Rita: "I called them last week when one of my CSR popped a few keys off her keyboard."

You: "Was she remote?"

Rita: "Yeah, and I gave her an earful. Anyway, the Help Desk team had the keyboard sent to her the same day!"

You: "I remember when it would take weeks to get a keyboard."

Gary: "What changed?"

Rita: "We fired Bob and hired the new lady, Patricia."

You: "Now now, we do not speak ill of the dead. But yes, Patricia is amazing."

Gary: "I called them yesterday to recover a file I deleted. They fixed it while I was still on the phone. The agent was super nice- we talked about fishing while the recovery took place."

You: "Can you imagine trying to work remotely with the old IT team?"

Rita: "Nope, it would have been hell."

This may sound like a ridiculous conversation, but your leadership does and will talk like this. If you are an IT leader reading this, they talk about you, they judge you, and when earned, they will praise you.

The experiences of this organization's leadership and their stories sound more like IT Heaven than IT Hell. Things still break, issues still happen, but the organization understands this will happen, and the Help Desk is a pleasure to work with when it does. How did this team get there? Take a look at the chapter list. Go ahead, we can wait……

Done looking? Great. Now, put them in reverse order. This is the order in which you must implement your Help Desk team. Work your way back out of the hells. If you are making a new IT team or rebuilding a broken one, start with the leader.

1. Hire a passionate, dedicated, and customer service-focused leader. If you're able to salvage the current leader, great. Just remember it is hard to "make someone care."
2. The leader must create and promote a culture of customer service focus, dedication, and passion.
3. The leader must hire, train, and, if needed, fire their staff to find like-minded and skilled individuals.
4. The leader must define, set, and uphold expectations with the organization and its team.
5. The leader must organize, coordinate, facilitate, and offer training to all employees.
6. The leader must work with their team and create a strong yet positive impression to be projected by their team.
7. The leader must be a steward of the IT expenditure and purchase the items that add to the team's success as a whole and avoid the expenditures that take away from that success.

"Tell me how to do this," you say. Well, the truth is, there is no one-size-fits-all solution to your team. You must look at the hells we have described here and use the laid out methods. You will not use 100% of the methods; a proficient IT leader will tweak approaches to best suit their team.

This is a constant effort. You will never get to a point and say, "my work is done." Making IT Heaven is a mindset. You will need to build and foster the growth of IT Saints, individuals who share your passion for making IT a partner of the organization. Here are ways to make your currently wonderful IT employees more saintly:

- Have them lead trainings for the non-IT employees.
- Send them to off-site training and conferences.
- Promote branding and team building.
- Celebrate and champion their achievements.

Have them lead trainings for the non-IT employees. This is the most powerful experience for any IT Help Desk agent. These are massive confidence and image builders. If your agents lead these classes with the "heart of a teacher," they set a foundation for strong relationships with the employees of the organization. The Help Desk agent also gains a better understanding of issues and questions the users face. Having this two-way understanding helps give each perspective on their needs, desires, and goals (read more in the chapter, "The Hell of an Uneducated Employee").

Send them to off-site training and conferences. These trips become fond and fun memories for your agents. They not only learn the presented material, but they also create connections and relationships with other IT professionals who face the same struggles and "IT Demons." These professional events provide additional resources for your agents to lean on when they come across new and more complicated issues, ultimately creating a tremendous sense of value in your agents. They begin to view themselves as an asset to the organization and that, in turn, the organization is vested in the agent's success and development (read more in the chapter, "The Hell of Hiring, Training, and Firing").

Promote branding and team building. Your team is a team, so treat them as such. Just as a fanatic for a sports team would wear jerseys and have branded gear, so should your team. Cheer for your team, and wear the gear with pride.

Build the camaraderie that comes with being a team. This must be a united, cultural shift for your colleagues (read more in the chapter, "The Hell of Culture").

Celebrate and champion their achievements. IT pros are often the shy, awkward nerd among nerds. They lack many social skills, most significantly, self-promotion. You must build up their confidence and self-image. This goes beyond simple recognition. If you have an agent develop something "cool" that makes the end user's life better or easier, arrange a time and forum for them to present this improvement to the greater organization. Beyond just promoting your agent's name, the organization will see that the IT team is actively working to improve IT quality for everyone (read more in the chapter, "The Hell of Impressions").

"How do I know it's working?" Metrics and message. You will see the backlog of tickets reduced, and you will hear from the organization directly how their view of the team has improved. You will hear from your team, "I like working here" and "this is fun." The organizational leadership will have time to smile and go to lunch knowing full well that IT is taken care of... that is true **IT Heaven.**

Below is a taste of heaven from the IT's team point of view:

You are the manager of the IT Help Desk. You spend most of your days working with the advanced IT teams on improving the technology environment. You do not spend much time in the "Technology" room as the team is self-sufficient, and you trust they are actively and efficiently assisting users. You are taking your team out for lunch to recognize a full quarter of more positive customer feedback scores than negative ones (a department first!). You let the team pick, and they choose a hibachi restaurant.

You are sitting at the cooktop with your team, and you take a moment to admire each and their progress.

Your senior team member, **Nick,** has made significant progress in dropping his catchphrase, "not my job." Now he says, "let me help" far more often, even if he carries some of the same attitudes. He has become a favorite of the CFO, which suits Nick just fine. Since you are paying, Nick has ordered the steak and lobster combo.

Nick's best buddy, **Steve,** has already finished his soup and salad and asks if anyone does not want theirs. Steve is wearing one of the polo shirts you purchased for the team. It's not tucked into his jeans (at least he's not in his sloppy sweat pants anymore). Not great, but it's a start. Steve actually enjoys walking the halls to help users (he found out that the CSR team always has candy). The sales team enjoys his energy, and he is having more fun every day.

Quiet at the end of the table is **Andy.** He gave Steve his salad and is sipping his Dr. Pepper. Andy may not look it here, but he is at home leading training classes. He especially enjoys training new employees during their introduction week. He has come out of his shell in so many ways: he has taken up a club sport, he hangs out with the team after work, and he even brought a date to the last group outing.

Your newest agent, **Patricia**, is chatting with the server and trying out the little Japanese she knows. You won't tell the other team, but she is quickly becoming your top agent. She is still under contract with the vendor, but you can for sure see her become permanent and perhaps even be your replacement someday.

Since the organization is paying for lunch, you decide to talk shop.

You: "Ok, team, thank you all for going to lunch with me."

Steve: "Thanks for paying!"

Nick: "Oh boy, I know this tone, here it comes."

You: "What tone?"

Andy: "The 'I want to ask you a question" tone."

You: "Do I have a tone? I guess I do, as I do have a question."

Patricia: "Let's hear it, boss."

Steve: "Yeah, we gotta work next weekend for a new build?"

You: "No, I had an ulterior motive for bringing you all here."

Nick: "I knew it."

You: "Nothing bad. I just wanted to have a neutral ground to ask you all… how am I doing? What can I do better?"

Silence hangs in the air for a moment. It breaks when Steve burps. The group burst out in laughter.

Patricia: "Oh man, Steve, that was gross."

Steve: "Excuse me."

You: "Anyway, seriously. How can I do better? Nick, surely you can think of something."

Nick: "You mean besides paying us more?"

Steve laughs way too loud.

You: "Yes, besides that."

Nick: "Really, not much. You keep the "shoulder taps" from rolling in. You point us toward the issues that matter. Best of all, you sort of leave us alone to do the work."

Steve: "Yeah, I agree. I do not feel nearly as busy since you took over. And all the food has been great."

Patricia: "What was it like before?"

Andy: "Endless calls, taps, and tickets."

Hell Desk To Help Desk

Patricia: "Endless?"

Steve: "Yeah, all day every day, just work rolling in."

Patricia: "What changed?"

Nick: "We got rid of Bob."

Steve: "Hear, hear!"

Patricia: "What was Bob like?"

Andy: "He was a boss, not a leader."

Patricia: "What do you mean?"

Nick: "He never helped, he never reviewed us, and he was never there."

Steve: "He never bought us food, he never did tickets, and he never even asked how we are doing."

Patricia: "Oh wow, so Hell?"

Andy: "Yeah…."

You: "How am I any better?"

Nick: "You are there, right in the trenches with us. When you're not in the office, we know you are out fighting the battles to help us. In fact, we made a nickname for you."

You: "For me?"

Steve: "Yeah, we dub you 'The Hammer!'"

You: "The Hammer?"

Andy: "We say there is an issue, and you make it go away!"

Nick: "You slap it down and we know it's gone. You hammer it!"

You: "And that is good?"

Patricia: "Yeah, I have never had a leader like you. You care about us, want us to succeed, and are just there for us. It really is **heaven**."

Ok, you can stop laughing. You are thinking there is no way the conversation happened. Well, it did, and it can happen for your IT leader too. What does this leader do? They lead. They are involved, active, and fully chasing down issues and 'hammering' them into oblivion. The leader is present. The team knows they are aware of their work and vested in making their work life more manageable. The leader does not quibble over days off or is a clock watcher who berates for not being in your chair at certain times. As long as the work is getting done and the users are happy, the Help Desk leader is happy.

This leader is not looking for the next promotion; they want to promote their team. They are not looking for glory but to glorify those under their leadership. They do not seek attention for themselves but to bring attention to the IT team's issues. The Help Desk leader approaches this from a love for their team perspective, not for themselves. This is the true key to all of this, a leader who is vested in their team's success and work/life balance. **Heaven for an IT team can be best described as "time."** Time to work on projects, to learn new skills, time to talk, time to breathe, time to enjoy their work.

If you find a respectful organization, a leader who is engaged, and an IT team that has time, *that* is **IT heaven.**

Index 1 – The IT Demons

AKA- Sometimes Far Too Real

Use this index as a quick guide to help you identify the IT Demons and to find techniques to exorcise them. Your demons will be unique, some will be a combination of two or three. These are general strategies for dealing with the demons we see over and over again in the IT world.

Sloppy Steve - Always a mess. T-shirts and sweatpants are the norm. Food is always close by. He is out of shape, so all work is an effort. He is often out sick. Focused on the next lunch or when work hours end.

You can help a Sloppy Steve with simple conversations. He will get his feelings hurt when you bring up his general appearance. Encourage him to dress up and celebrate (not sarcastically) when he does. Encourage him to lead a training session and have him "dress like a professor." Leaders, you must lead by example. Your employees will never be more presentable then you are. The chapter, "The Hell of Impressions" goes into deeper detail on Sloppy Steve.

Awkward Andy - This is the classic stereotype of the IT nerd. A lesser demon as they are often fine at their job, but just really painful to be around and socialize with. They often embarrass themselves and the organization with their inability to just act human.

There is a good chance Andy is a good IT employee. This is the one that is often the most fun to work with. Have them lead training, meetings, and presentations. Simply encourage them to present themselves to the world and, as a leader, be a strong encouragement of their strengths and worth. They will grow in confidence and enhance their skillset. In fact, these Andy's often become a Perfect Patrick. The chapter of "The Hell of Culture" highlights more ways to help an Andy.

Not My Job Nick - Always has an excuse to avoid work. He knows his duties and the duties of everyone else. Will work stringently within the guidelines of his job description, down to every last bullet point. Knows what time it is and what time he is done with work. Usually openly wonders why he is not in charge.

This is the most nefarious of the demons and will be the hardest to exorcise. He will be combative and aggressively lazy. You address this demon with data, expectations, perspectives, and positive exposure. He will say, "It's Not My Job." Prove him otherwise. Assault him with data, "Nick, you must close 500 tickets a month, and you have been averaging 200." Once he meets the numbers, switch tactics to customer experience. Implement a solid feedback system and weekly review of his customer service metrics. Customers are far happier if a single tech can solve all their issues and Nicks are famous for handing off users to other techs. Phase three of the exorcism is peer evaluations. Have your team, who we guarantee is tired of Nick too, be open about how his unwillingness to help is affecting them. This can be done privately, but we recommend utilizing open, round tables and having the team share their frustrations in a structured way. Lastly, give him the "fame" these demons always desire. Have him work directly with senior organizational leadership on their issues. Have him lead sessions and training that give him lots of attention and exposure. Every chapter addresses Nick and his ways.

Bob the Boss - This is the IT boss of demons. A Bob usually does not have any IT skills. They are often just placed in this role as no one else was available, and the organization did not want him anywhere else. Bob has no love for IT, he only loves being a "boss." He is looking for that next raise, that next promotion.

If your Bob has some IT skills, we must find and unlock them to ignite his unkindled love for IT. He needs to be reminded about the joy the job can bring. Encourage him to get his hands dirty and help on projects, to work some tickets, to once again take part in the actual work of IT support. If your Bob has no IT background, the best way to fix this Bob is to fire and replace, or have him **read this book and transform!**

Index 2 – The Non-IT Demons

You know who we are talking about.

Good Enough Gary - Usually a non-IT team member. Why spend money when things are working today? This demon does not understand IT demands and will always fight to reserve money. They will point to old hardware and say, "why not use that?" Loves to say, "We never needed this before."

Confront Gary with worst-case scenarios. Ask him, "If this goes down, how much money will we lose?" Help Gary understand that we need to invest in stability to prevent losses. Read more on Gary in "The Hell of IT Expenditure."

Ignorant Isaac - "Computers can do that?" This is the employee who has somehow survived the 21st century and never used their phone to play music. This demon is not only oblivious to technology, but they are violently repulsed by the idea that they do not understand it. If you attempt to educate, beware, they will lash out.

Isaacs can be tricky. Directly confronting them is never the answer. Isaacs needs to feel like they, themselves, found the answer to their problem. Have your most customer service-focused agent ready to become best friends with Isaac and build a bond of trust. Once the bond is built, Isaac will let the agent "teach him some tricks." Education is the key to exorcising an Isaac. The chapter, "The Hell of an Uneducated Employee," goes over ways to battle an Isaac.

Right Now Rita - Fix it now! This is the demon of expectations. Rita loves to tell you how much money it is costing the company that she can't read her emails.

Rita is the hardest demon to placate when work and life aren't running perfectly. A good IT leader will be able to talk with emotional intelligence and understanding of her perspective. She cannot be spoken to with numbers, but with feelings and clearly defined expectations and goals. Let her know what you plan to do and how long it is expected to take.

Index 3 – The IT Saints

AKA - People who simply do not exist.

Saint Patrick the Perfect - Knows every piece of technology the organization has and uses. Always wears a tie and a very clean, spiffy outfit. Hair and hygiene are exceptional. His work area is immaculate. Always smiling, always offering to help. Able to speak to users and lead trainings. Leadership knows them by name and usually asks directly for their assistance on issues. Never calls out sick, never says no to requests, never leaves for lunch. Works late, comes in early, and never complains.

To be honest, what is described here is not what you want. Never leaves for lunch? Preposterous! Let them go to lunch and enjoy a break. The truth is, anyone can be a "Perfect Patrick/Patricia." They could be a leader, an agent, a developer, or anything in between. The saint may not "look the part," but they are passionate about helping your users. They are customer service-focused and patient. Their desire to improve IT for all is contagious. Like any perfect "saint," they evangelize good IT.

Sometimes, the best saints are demon conversions. Here are some techniques you can use to convert the demons you find into saints:

Awkward Andy into an **Awesome Andy**- This is the easiest of the demon conversions. Andys are often the most technology talented and skilled agent on your team. Their only "sins" are normally shyness and a lack of self-confidence.

Have Andys lead trainings, present technology to the organization, and attend public speaking classes like Toastmasters. An Andy can be a fantastic agent if only they speak out a little more.

Sloppy Steve into a **Stellar Steve**- Steves often lack IT skills, as well as basic hygiene. It comes back to a general laziness in the individual. For conversion of a Steve, we have seen success in encouraging and developing their self-image. They often just need their self-confidence built. Many leaders have had Steve pair up with a confident, well-dressed agent and we see Steve picking up the style choices and behaviors of this model agent.

Not My Job Nick into a **Nurturing Nick** - Nicks can be a tricky conversion. They are usually skilled at technology and may often be your most advanced agent. To make this conversion happen, you need to find where the "not my job mentality" comes from. For some, it is a feeling of being "better" than the task. For others, it comes from pure laziness. If the motivation is to rise above the work, you need to find ways to challenge Nick with automations and system enhancements. If laziness is the driving force, you need to find Nick's passion. Talk to him and see what he loves, what motivates and excites him. He may be jaded on IT work now, but this was not always the case. Find that carrot to lead him into the work you identify. Bend this passion around the work that needs to be done. Nicks want to lead; use this and turn them into a trainer for your IT team and the organization as a whole.

Index 4 – References

Backing up our points

1. https://news.microsoft.com/en-nz/2018/10/16/true-cost-of-not-replacing-computers-revealed-in-microsoft-study-more-than-4000-each
2. https://www.forbes.com/sites/steveandriole/2017/06/21/digital-ignorance-in-government-better-call-justin-about-quantum-computing-and-barack-about-ai/?sh=2d674f344245
3. http://www3.weforum.org/docs/GITR2016/WEF_GITR_United_States_2016.pdf
4. https://nymag.com/intelligencer/2016/11/our-ignorance-about-technology-is-dangerous-and-embarrassing.html
5. https://blogs.scientificamerican.com/news-blog/ignorance-not-bliss-when-it-comes-t-2009-04-17/
6. https://www.pewresearch.org/internet/2017/08/10/theme-3-trust-will-not-grow-but-technology-usage-will-continue-to-rise-as-a-new-normal-sets-in/
7. https://www.mhanational.org/work-life-balance
8. https://www.techrepublic.com/article/talking-shop-when-is-a-help-desk-call-really-an-emergency/
9. https://www.britannica.com/technology/Moores-law/
10. https://www.redpoints.com/blog/hard-facts-about-software-piracy/
11. https://www.washingtonpost.com/news/the-switch/wp/2018/04/10/transcript-of-mark-zuckerbergs-senate-hearing/

12. https://www.paloaltonetworks.com/blog/2021/06/the-cost-of-cybersecurity-incidents-the-problem/
13. https://www.howtogeek.com/173760/htg-explains-why-does-rebooting-a-computer-fix-so-many-problems/

Index 5 – Further Reading

We asked IT leaders what books they recommend. Here is a sampling of books that came up multiple times:

We recommend this book for all leaders, not just IT leaders.
- Start with Why: How Great Leaders Inspire Everyone to Take Action - Simon Sinek

An essential read for all employees.
- Emotional Intelligence - Daniel Goleman

A guide to help leaders find that "one metric" we ask you to look for in the chapter, "The Hell of Leadership."
- Measure What Matters: How Google, Bono, and the Gates Foundation Rock the World with OKRs - John Doerr

A great read for anyone in IT on improving your organization by using the dev-ops cycle.
- The Phoenix Project: A Novel about IT, DevOps, and Helping Your Business Win - Gene Kim, Kevin Behr, George Spafford

A guide for leaders to find ways of motivating their team through change.
- The Carrot Principle - Adrian Gostick, Chester Elton

Look for future books in The Hell Desk series at https://helldeskbooks.com/

About the Author

Brian P McCoppin has been a senior leader and innovator in IT for over twenty years. He has led transformation after transformation of IT support within numerous industries, both government and private, large and small, established and newly opened. He currently works as a senior IT leader for a Fortune 500 company, lives in Florida with his wife and three kids, and spends his non-IT time working on his boat and practicing Tang Soo Do.

Continue your IT Salvation online.

https://helldeskbooks.com/

- Find more resources
- Join our mailing list and community
- Share and read stories of IT transformation
- Listen to podcasts
- Watch videos
- Locate live events
- Schedule a consultation with an IT Evangelist

www.ingramcontent.com/pod-product-compliance
Lightning Source LLC
Chambersburg PA
CBHW071511220526
45472CB00003B/984